ALL IN

An Educator's Manual for Winning
Hearts, Minds, and High Performance
by Intentionally Leading School Culture

Kelsey LaVigne

HIGHPOINT
ACADEMIC

This edition published by Highpoint Academic
For information, write to info@highpointpubs.com.

First Edition

ISBN: 978-1-7372886-8-8

Library of Congress Cataloging-in-Publication Data

LaVigne
All In
An Educator's Manual for Winning Hearts, Minds, and High Performance by Intentionally Leading School Culture

Summary: *"This book explains in detail how Brilla Charter Schools cultivated an unbeatable culture of resilience, illuminating its unique story on how any school, public or private, can build a vision-driven culture in pursuit of high performance, engaged clients and committed talent."* – Provided by publisher.

ISBN: 978-1-7372886-8-8 (hardcover)
1.Education: Administration

Library of Congress Control Number: 2022907623

Cover and Interior Design by Sarah M. Clarehart

Manufactured in the United States of America

To all Brilla Cardinals, past, present, and future.

At a Glance

My story and how I came to think about culture in this way—a shout-out
to Walt Disney, the University of Southern California, and Jim Fay.
Suggestions to frame your encounter with the content of this book.

You can't make anyone do anything, so you must compel them, both
rationally and emotionally. The vehicle is culture. When a leader combines
intentional culture with an effective program model, results follow.

PART 1: VISION

Practices for building culture must be applied in service of something:
your vision. Put it on paper, appeal to the senses, and immerse yourself
in the details.

Craft differentiated, strategically timed communications to consistently
reinforce your vision for each stakeholder group. Clarity and transparency
are required to earn commitment.

Leverage sensory cues—from symbols and colors to rituals and common
language—to reinforce membership in the special thing that is your vision.

PART 2: ENGAGEMENT

Education is a people-driven business. Create the conditions of connection among students, families, and staff to strengthen their commitment to each other, especially for the darkest days when the vision alone isn't enough to engender full commitment.

Invite stakeholders to feel a cascading sense of ownership for the organizational vision by providing legitimate opportunities to influence, uplift, and participate in it, and by setting interdependent goals.

An inclusive vision must be rooted in celebrations of human dignity, ensuring that the vision has a place for all stakeholders to feel genuinely welcome to both connect and participate.

PART 3: EXECUTION

Building systems in explicit support of the vision needs to be a preoccupation of leadership, from the anticipation phase of launching an initiative to reliving its successful implementation.

A coherent operational strategy is one in which all types of resources—particularly time, budget, and recognition—are deployed with visible intentional support for the vision and an eye toward balance and prioritization.

Results are facilitated through people. Ensure every element of the cultivation, selection, and performance management of talent will be in service of your vision.

Reflections on other lessons learned from implementing these practices, and a final word of encouragement and caution.

Contents

PART 3: EXECUTION

Foreword

In 2014 I failed an interview. It was my Brilla culture interview with Kelsey LaVigne, the author of this book.

In my defense, failing was not entirely my fault—how was I supposed to know that, in a *job interview*, your response to the question: "What's your dream job?" should have been something "awesome and juicy." Replying "lawyer" was a totally unacceptable response. Or that when asked "What animal are you?" your response—not just what you said, but also *how* you responded—was in fact completely indicative of your character and of what kind of employee and colleague you would be.

One week after that interview I met Kelsey for the second time. It was my first day of work at Brilla College Prep Elementary School in the Mott Haven neighborhood of the South Bronx. I walked into a construction zone on the first floor and entered a dust-filled classroom that had been declared the summer office for administrative staff. A few minutes after I arrived a woman wearing sneakers, a high ponytail, and a Brilla T-shirt walked in. I quickly recognized her as the woman who had asked me all those bizarre questions the week before. Kelsey re-introduced herself as the Assistant Principal and Director of Community and Culture. She sat down at her computer and never looked up until she took a break to make lunch.

At the time, I did not realize I was watching a genius at work. I was seeing the inventor of Brilla's magic. Kelsey was busy envisioning a new kind of school culture and bringing it to life. In that moment she was creating joy, love, emotions, bonds, a brand, an altogether intangible recipe that has aged well even as it continues to evolve.

In the following months and years, I got to know Kelsey through her work. While Kelsey was not officially in charge at the beginning of my first year at Brilla she may as well have been. She kept everyone on track, letting staff know what to care about, and when and how to show up for students and for one another. She knew when to wear a tutu and a wig, when to wear a bright red Cardinal costume, when to arrive early or stay late to celebrate or support a colleague, family, a scholar.

Working at Brilla in 2014 was like doing the most important work in the world while being at a party. It was like being challenged intellectually while being in Disney World.

For the first time in my professional career, I felt like I was being held to high standards that actually mattered. Kelsey's standards. Standards of personal and mutual accountability. Standards of how to show you truly care for people—all people. Kelsey knew that kids do not learn from people they don't like,[1] and that the adults working in a school are no different. She knew that if work was a place where people can be themselves and feel valued, they will show up and bring all their gifts.

---

[1] Ted Talks, "Every Kid Needs a Champion," Rita F. Pierson, https://www.ted.com/talks/rita_pierson_every_kid_needs_a_champion?language=en

It took me a little while to acclimate to this outgoing woman who cared about everything—where the dishes in the lounge went, whether or not there should be printers in the teachers' lounge, how classroom furniture was arranged, how and when and where families received mail and flyers, what colors those flyers should be, what photos went on what walls, which boards should or should not have butcher paper, and which shades of red were Nebraska-red and which were Brilla-red. There was no detail too small, and no obstacle too large for Kelsey.

When Brilla's founding principal announced his departure, I recall the audible gasp in the room. And I recall how just as quickly we sighed in relief and cheered for the person who would be taking the reins: Kelsey.

During that transition period there were times when Kelsey felt she had lost her dream job. But the rest of us knew Kelsey's impact was only growing and becoming further reaching. She was in the driver's seat because, to a degree no one else could access, Kelsey understood why Brilla meant "shine."

Kelsey spent her first year as Brilla's sole leader living out what, years later, would become known as Brilla's Essential Practices. Kelsey took good people and led them. I mean truly led them. She saw who needed to be softened, who needed to be pushed, who needed to be motivated, who needed to be empowered, who needed to be brought in, who needed competition, who needed love, and she did it all.

Kelsey created a team and a vision for what Brilla Schools have become: a place where students, families, and staff feel part of something larger than themselves, and where their sense of self changes permanently and positively.

I know Kelsey did that for me. And that's coming from someone who failed her culture interview.

— Alexandra Apfel, Former Brilla Principal, New York City
Charter Schools Center, Inclusive Education Specialist

Preface

When the COVID-19 pandemic swept across the world in 2020, educators found themselves in an unfamiliar place. They were on the front line of a public-health emergency. In the spring of 2020 schools across the United States closed. Remote learning abruptly became the norm, disrupting the lives of countless kids and families. In underresourced areas of the country, places like the neighborhood where I work, the disruption was especially marked.

In most of the country the situation was hardly better when the new school year began in September 2020. Right behind the COVID-19 virus itself, the biggest barrier to reopening was that so many students, families, and even staff did not trust school leaders to look out for the health of both their minds and their bodies. Some school systems did not fully open and resume in-person learning for another twelve months!

Yet that same September, Brilla Public Charter Schools, which I helped found in 2013, reopened with 60 percent of families selecting in-person learning and 99 percent of staff reporting in person for work. (Brilla is pronounced bree-ya. In Spanish the word means "shine.") And even prior to Brilla's remarkable in-person reopening, in August 2020, when Brilla was still fully remote and many students and families at other schools were simply not showing up for remote learning[1], Brilla maintained a daily network-wide student attendance rate of over 90 percent.

What made Brilla different? The difference was that our community—our staff, our students, our families, even our authorizers—had learned to trust us and to count on the fact that every choice we make, and every choice we have always made, is intentional and in support of Brilla's vision: the holistic development of children.

The pandemic revealed the importance of a strong, vision-driven organizational culture to motivate stakeholder buy-in and commitment when the going gets tough. Schools are facing extreme staff resignations and turnover at all times throughout the school year.[2] Students and families have checked out. But Brilla has proved resilient during these tough times. Brilla's culture proved to be the motivational glue to keep staff, students, and families showing up and trusting the organization.

This was no accident. As this book reveals, Brilla's culture is the result of many years of hard, thoughtful work. Before the pandemic revealed the perils of treating culture as an afterthought, Brilla's culture had earned renown. Since its beginnings in 2013 Brilla has intentionally cultivated a culture in which families, staff, and students invest in a shared vision for the school and for each other. By the time

---

[1] Jessica Winter, "Even as Omicron Wanes, New York City's Teachers Are in a Holding Pattern," The New Yorker, January 20, 2022

[2] Michael Sainato, "'Exhausted and Underpaid': Teachers across the US Are Leaving Their Jobs in Numbers," *The Guardian*, October 4, 2021.

the COVID-19 crisis hit, we had replicated that culture across three different Brilla campuses in the Bronx, and we were about to do it at two more. Our growth as a public charter school attracted attention.

And rightly so. The stats speak for themselves. As of the 2020-2021 school year, 80 percent staff retention, single-digit midyear staff resignations, zero expulsions, third-in-state literacy and math state exam results among schools with comparable student populations, 60+ percent proficiency in math and ELA, 100 percent family attendance at parent-teacher conferences, 99 percent parent satisfaction, and student retention rates of 90 percent. These statistics are even more impressive in light of Brilla's success at serving all learners, including special populations, which as of June 2021 accounted for over 20 percent of the student body.

Why I wrote this book.

Why did I write this book? Because we have been repeatedly asked how to replicate a strong culture like Brilla's. Schools and leaders have always been interested in Brilla's "secret sauce," but that interest, for the most part, has been passive. Other priorities are eventually elevated over cultivating and leading strong culture. All of a sudden, the pandemic has shown the perils of not elevating culture to a primary organizational priority. The pandemic has revealed clearly that organizational culture is no longer a "nice to have." It has shown what we have always known at Brilla—culture is integral to student achievement.

I have attempted to provide in these pages a manual for envisioning, cultivating, and leading an intentional culture that will result in sustained buy-in and high performance from all stakeholders in your organization.

Though most of the culture concepts that follow are illustrated with examples from my experience at Brilla, my thinking about these concepts was shaped by earlier life experiences.

I grew up in Georgia. When applying to colleges, I applied to a handful of colleges in the Southeast. The outlier was the University of Southern California. My sole reason for applying was a family connection to Los Angeles. A purely sentimental interest, in other words, with minimal intention behind it.

What I noticed right away was that the recruiting materials I got from USC came with stickers that had my name on them. Even without calling it as such I noticed this small recognition of my individual dignity. I was impressed not by USC's personalization but by its intentionality. The stickers signaled that USC wanted me to be part of their thing.

When I visited the campus for an interview, I could not help noticing that everyone I passed seemed to be wearing USC swag, athletes and cinema majors alike. Cardinal red was everywhere. The sense of everyone's connection to USC was palpable—literally palpable in the sense that one could touch it. There was a pride about the place that made me want to be part of it.

Like most eighteen-year-olds I did not know what I wanted to do with my life, but I quickly discovered that the USC Marshall School of Business was offering a spring break trip to Shanghai. That decided it. I was a business major.

On that degree track, leadership development was my concentration. I took courses in designing and leading teams, marketing, and the art of persuasion. I am the first to admit that this was not the conventional trajectory of a future educator. It turned out to be invaluable to the career I did not know I was going to choose.

A key part of being a business major at USC is Marshall's Experiential Learning Center. The mission of the ELC is to promote learning through doing. Students drive their own education by participating in application-based sessions on topics like group decision-making, problem solving, creating presentations, and conducting negotiations. It was fascinating stuff. We received immediate feedback by, among other methods, reviewing video of ourselves in action.

You could say that the intention of experiential learning is to help students absorb ideas at a molecular level, to feel less like they are acted upon and more like they are shaping the outcome in which they will share a part. It was a crucial lesson for my later career at Brilla. It was a path to understanding not just concepts but their consequences. It was one more lesson in intentionality. All of it would be central to my formation as an educator.

Meanwhile, I was having another kind of experience that in its own way was not far removed from what I was learning at ELC. This other experience was USC's Joint Educational Project. If there was a single spark that lit my interest in education, JEP was it.

Founded in 1972, JEP is among the largest service-learning programs in the United States. More than two thousand USC students enroll in its work-study and volunteer programs every year—almost 5 percent of the total student population.

JEP partners with local schools in the surrounding community. At the school where I was assigned I taught geology to a group of middle school students. I developed my curriculum from what I was learning in my own geology class at USC.

In comparison with the local Los Angeles communities that surround it, USC can seem like an oasis of privilege. JEP gave me my first close-up look at how wealth disparity influences educational outcomes.

Several older peers I was acquainted with through JEP became interested in the education field as well. After graduation they joined Teach for America, a nonprofit organization dedicated to strengthening educational equity and excellence. As I recall, none of them were education majors. They were communications majors, pre-med, political science—a real hodgepodge of career interests. That sort of mélange is a big part of TFA's philosophy: Attract people who can come at the challenge of educational inequities from multiple directions to create a cadre of advocates for education reform.

When I graduated in 2009, I enlisted in Teach for America for what I thought would be a standard two-year hitch. I had no idea I would spend the next decade founding and building a school system from the ground up.

Teach for America placed me in a Brooklyn charter school. On day one, after a month-long prep course in how to teach, I was thrown into the deep end of the pool, just the kids and me. Luckily I am a big believer in learning from mistakes, because I made plenty.

I was forced to transform from a business major into a fifth grade math teacher. As any school administrator knows, if hiring is hard, then hiring math and science teachers is harder. This is especially true in underresourced school communities. It is a fact of life that not enough teachers want to work where kids and the schools they attend are struggling. Supports are limited, pay is low, turnover is high.[3] The gift of Teach for America is in providing schools in underresourced communities with access to a pool of talent that is not only capable but interested—talent that wants the challenge because it is demanding and meaningful work.

By the time a Teach for America candidate gets to a job interview they have already been so well vetted that a school can have a high degree of confidence that even without fully developed teaching chops (which certainly described me), the candidate has shown evidence of resilience and an ability to power through tough situations (which I was about to need in abundance). Doing anything for the first time is hard, and my first year as a paid teacher was certainly a test of both my teaching chops and my resilience.

Managing my class that first year was the most difficult part. The kids liked me, but they knew they could get away with things that they could not with other teachers in the building. Pretty soon I was called into the principal's office.

---

[3] See, for example, "The Teacher Shortage, 2021 Edition." Based on a survey of 1,200 school and district leaders across the United States by Frontline Education, the study found that districts in all settings—rural, suburban, and urban—are struggling with talent issues. Teacher shortages are most common in urban school systems, with 75 percent of districts in cities of any size reporting teacher shortages.

"It is not going well," my principal said. Points for being direct, I guess. Our conversation boiled down to this: fix your performance or get fired.

It was a terrifying moment. I was renting an apartment I could barely afford. The school was funding my master's program; if I lost my job, I would have to pay it all back. I was given a performance improvement plan. I got some extra coaching, and that was a help. If nothing else, it showed someone was rooting for me to succeed.

Before the year was over I pulled myself out of my tailspin. At a later performance review my principal said, "You have made improvement, but we are not sure you have bought into our culture." I was not sure either.

By "culture" the school meant its discipline systems. The message to me was "You are not holding the kids accountable for misbehavior." The kids who passed through my math class were so fixated on the discipline system that if I asked them what kind of day they had, they would reply by telling me how many disciplinary demerits they got.

Something every teacher in every school must contend with, especially in the lower grades, is that it is difficult work to influence tiny humans who are not yet fully rational. That is exactly the reason some schools fall into the trap of overfocusing on rewards and consequences. In that first year I overcorrected. I recall one class period when I gave twenty-three demerits to only eighteen kids. It only took three demerits over the course of a day to get an automatic detention. I was proud of myself that day; in retrospect, it was despicable.

Kids bring so much to school that a teacher cannot control. In the shock of my first year as a teacher, I began thinking hard about the thing a teacher can control. That thing is culture, which can be deliberately shaped.

The effects of building a school culture using prescribed rewards and penalties are short-lived. Rewards and penalties are a system to be gamed. Kids learn to be good at the game. It was evident to me pretty quickly that there are far more lasting effects to be gained from finding a way into students—into their heads, into their hearts, into their lives outside of school. In other words, to inspire them, to engage with content and spark a hunger to learn, and to cultivate the feeling that when they are in our classroom, they are part of something. Those are the things that prompt high performance.

During the purgatory of my first-year performance improvement plan I remember sitting in on another teacher's class. He seemed to be a master at leading and managing his classroom. But it was not explained to me how he did that. All I could conclude was that he had been given some gift from above. Or maybe he had developed a set of instincts that only came with more experience than I had.

It took me a while to learn that no teacher can make kids do anything. The best teachers, I noticed, hardly ever had to use the systems of rewards and punishments that preoccupy too many schools. The best teachers use influence to get the kids into learning. Their classrooms were a culture unto themselves.

Whatever my personal struggles during my first year of teaching, I was learning the elements of a vision-driven culture. I was learning how to create a classroom where students want to be. And I was forming my ideas for applying these insights to school culture as a whole—to the kids, first of all, but also to families and staff.

For example, in my second year (after my reputation had improved a little bit), I volunteered to help with our school's weekly pep rally. We blew up the established framework of our pep rallies. (Pro tip: get science teachers involved. They are masters of spectacle. Kids love it.) Later we created what we called the Culture Club to oversee all our school events.

Culture Club taught me a lesson I have never forgotten, a lesson that will be a bright thread throughout this book. That lesson was the centrality of winning the full participation of every member of the school community in realizing the vision. Every member of the staff had to pick a Culture Club event committee to join and help out. That was key to buy-in and to mutual accountability.

As intentional as we tried to be, the unintended consequence of Culture Club was how it turned out to be a way of giving joy to teachers and staff.

At the end of my second year I wrote a proposal for a job I was calling culture lead—someone who thinks about all the things a school can do right to shape the way kids—and staff—experience school. A year later, culture lead was part of my actual job.

I was beginning to test the limits of my span of influence as a teacher-leader. For instance, I did not have the capacity to influence the family experience beyond what extended directly from my classroom. Unless I was able to influence the system of a school, there would never be the opportunity to create an intentional culture with the depth and dimension that would lead to fulfillment for students, families, and staff alike.

In 2012, one of my colleagues from Teach for America, another former business major named Aaron Gillaspie, received a fellowship from Seton Education Partners to open Brilla College Prep in the Mott Haven neighborhood of the Bronx.

Seton is an organization that developed in response to the closing of hundreds of Roman Catholic parochial schools in urban areas in the past two decades. Seton's mission is to continue serving the same population as those closed schools, most of whom are Latino and Black students.

Seton's vision is of what it calls "a classical education that nurtures the mind, body and soul while honoring the legitimate role of families as the first educators." What Seton and Aaron had in mind for Brilla was a K–8 public charter school in "the classical tradition"—a school where character would be lauded alongside achievement in academics. This would help students to grow intellectually, socially, and physically into people of good character and spirit. Brilla would prepare students for excellence in high school, in college, and in their life beyond formal education.

Pretty ambitious.

Seton secured a charter and funding. Later it inherited a shuttered school building that had formerly been a parochial school run by the Catholic Archdiocese of New York. Brilla was scheduled to open in September 2013. But in 2012 there were no students, no teachers, and no families who had ever heard of a Brilla school. Aaron was trying to recruit families and staff to get behind something that did not exist.

Recruiting students to Brilla took tremendous effort. Aaron moved to an apartment in the South Bronx. Everywhere he went in the neighborhood he kept an eye out for kids who looked like they might be four years old. He would strike up a conversation with their parents and tell them about the charter school that was opening the next September. He would tell them it was going to be amazing. And he would have them fill out an application then and there and take it with him.[4]

In Aaron's personal network were two friends who had the advantage of speaking Spanish, an immense value-add in the Mott Haven community. Samantha Martinez was a teacher looking for exactly the kind of challenge Aaron was proposing. Gerson Martinez was making a move from a career in finance to education. Aaron, Samantha, and Gerson made themselves visible in the Mott Haven neighborhood. The winter before Brilla opened you could find them standing on street corners engaging passersby and collecting applications. They set up tables in front of community centers and churches. That was how Brilla recruited families.

While they were still in launch mode Aaron pitched the school's board of directors on the idea of a director of community and culture for Brilla. I was the person he had in mind to fill that role. He had partnered with me on culture initiatives at our former school in Brooklyn, and believed in what I could offer as a founding member of the Brilla team. He described our vision of a school that was truly a community, where joy was baked into the culture and ethos, a school that would

---

[4] Leo Flores, "Young Entrepreneur Goes from Classroom to Boardroom," *Chron*, October 1, 2015.

have a lasting impact on kids throughout their lives. The board liked the idea and signed on.

As a result, I was one of Brilla's earliest hires.

Brilla attracted staff from a rich pool of talent. Teach for America came through with stellar rookie teachers. One of them went on to serve as founding principal of our first-ever middle school. Largely through word of mouth and personal networks, we attracted teachers looking for something different and willing to take a risk that would have been uncomfortable for many people. There were plenty of jobs available at other schools that first year. But our founding team wanted the job Brilla was offering.

So did I. And good thing, too. After year one, I found myself leading the organization. Aaron moved out of state, and I was promoted to principal of the flagship Brilla school. As the organization grew beyond one campus, so did my role. Over the next eight years, I helped lead the organization as head of schools, then superintendent, and ultimately chief of schools. During that time, we grew from one school in a secondhand building to five campuses across the South Bronx. My experiences in those years inform every page of the manual you are holding in your hands.

Central to my experiences at Brilla has been the power of a vision. You will hear me say repeatedly in this book that Brilla's vision does not need to be your vision. But in bringing school culture to life, being able to say what you want your school to be—first to yourself and then to your community—is an indispensable element.

Brilla was a start-up. Being entrepreneurial is our nature.

And in its early days Brilla certainly did its share of improvisation. But from the start we embraced process and knew that our approach to building our school had to be rigorous. We had made promises to families who were betting their children's education on us; the stakes were high. From our beginnings we have been codifying our approach to building a successful school. With every year that goes by we adapt, and then we codify the adaptation.

Though the specific audience for *All In* is educators, this codification and the lessons we have learned about a vision-driven, people-centered approach to high performance will be of value to any organization with the ambition to be exceptional.

Certainly these include educators in the steadily growing number of charter schools in the United States—three million students in nearly six thousand schools at last count. But it will also be of value to the 140,000 public schools across the United States that share in common with charters the strategic need to win staff commitment, full family involvement, and, above anything else, student achievement.

All In is designed to be used by educators desiring to elevate their outcomes by appealing to every individual's craving for purpose and desire for human connection, whether it is a teacher leading students in a classroom or an administrator leading a school team.

You do not have to take my word for it that a vision-driven culture drives high performance by winning hearts and minds. Look at the data. In 2018–2019—the pre-COVID-19 year—Brilla students sat in person for New York State reading and math exams and ranked third among schools with similar populations of students, whether they were multilanguage learners, students with disabilities, or economically disadvantaged students.

I am well aware of the criticism that charter schools seek to counsel out students who pull down their performance rankings. Here is something you need to know from the start. Brilla students enter via lottery. Their parents select us. Their children—every single one of them— are ours to cherish until they graduate or choose to leave. We have had zero expulsions in our history. Zero. And our retention rate, both for the general student population and special populations, is consistently 90 percent or higher (and that is despite the substantial swings in migration that COVID-19 triggered in 2020).

Each school year we survey families to assess their satisfaction with the job we are doing. We ask if enrolled families would recommend Brilla to other parents; 99 percent either agree or strongly agree.

Since our founding year, attendance at family conferences has been 100 percent—even during the pandemic, when our families Zoomed in from across time zones and from several continents. Literally, not one single family has ever missed a conference over the past eight years.

These results are facilitated through our incredible staff, whom we retain at roughly 80 percent, with limited instances of mid-year turnover.

And these numbers hold across all of our campuses—further evidence that a vision-driven culture can be methodically applied and replicated in the pursuit of high performance. That is what it means to be all in.

In the following pages I will offer a step-by-step approach to aligning vision with the choices that school leaders make every day. But first, let me frame what you are about to experience.

How this book is structured.

All In is not meant to be read once and put up on a shelf. I hope that it will end up dog-eared, scribbled upon, and argued about. Above all, *All In* is not meant to be read in solitude. That would be the antithesis of the book's core idea of full participation among every stakeholder in the realization of a vision.

You will notice that the three core sections of this manual— "Vision," "Engagement," and "Execution"—are each broken into three steps. These are more or less sequential in building a vision-driven school. Bear in mind as you read them that the work of creating a thriving school culture is never done. These steps will need revisiting all the time. There will always be other things vying for the attention of our hearts and minds. There is no "one and done" in leading a vision-centered school.

Each of these steps is introduced by an example from outside the field of education that illustrates the chapter's principal message. These examples might be drawn from NASA, the business sector, the military, sports—anywhere, really. The point these small stories make is that the steps described in this book for building a vision-centered culture are nearly universal precepts.

Peppered throughout each chapter are other examples drawn from our experience at Brilla. Bear in mind that the lessons of these examples are intended to be transferrable. We might illustrate a practice with a story about running a professional development workshop, for example, but the broader guidance that story provides should be equally applicable to putting on a community-building event. We might choose an example involving families to illustrate a concept, but the concept is equally applicable to students and staff. Most examples are drawn from experiences with school culture in a broad sense but can also be applied to classroom culture, the culture of a specific school team, etc. Remain open to make the content work for you and your context.

An admonition that you will read again and again in *All In* is to tell the members of your school community—and then to tell them again—what they are signing up for when they join your team. With that in mind, each chapter is introduced by a page describing what you sign up for when you begin to read.

At the end of each chapter the practices become actionable. You will encounter a set of questions intended to help you assess your current implementation of each practice in your specific context. The goal is to test whether or not your current school design and systems are supporting the realization of your vision and building a culture that supports it. Think of the questions as a brainstorming diagnostic. The reflection is meant to be a collaborative tool used by teams, not a solitary meditation used by a leader sitting all alone.

Part 1, "Vision," lays out the ways in which an intentionally developed vision informs every aspect of what is too often loosely called culture.

In too many organizations, not just schools, the conception of what culture means to the fulfilment of a vision is comparatively passive, something over which the members of the organization have no real control. That is wrong. Therefore, after we describe the "why" of culture in the introduction, we launch into the "Vision" section. Here we present crafting, communicating, and reinforcing a clear vision as distinct practices that are foundational to engaging hearts and minds.

The vision is the North Star that every subsequent decision or action (both manifestations of culture) is held up against. Precisely because this is an ongoing effort rather than a step reserved for start-up or founding, it is never too late to begin applying these practices. A school can learn to name out loud and in public its intention to build a culture that supports the realization of a detailed vision, and reinforce it constantly through intentional signaling.

We briefly describe key elements of the vision we have for Brilla Schools to give you context for the experience from which this book's insights are derived. These are not meant as an argument that you should adopt Brilla's vision. On the contrary, individual schools need to develop a vision distinctive to their specific mission and school community, with its specific needs and aspirations.

What is transferrable among all schools is the requirement of clarity in the vision and the intention to realize it everywhere, every day. As famed restauranteur Danny Meyer contends in his saltshaker theory of leadership, a leader's job is to "to teach everyone who works for us to distinguish center from off center"[5]—essentially, to know the vision.

Part 2, "Engagement," is a detailed tour of the mechanics behind organizing a school's structures to maximize connection and participation in service of the vision, with an acknowledgment that neither of these conditions can be authentically achieved without the precondition of inclusivity—accepting all the gifts. The strategic rationale for engagement is the same for schools as it is for any organization: a shared sense of purpose and a sincere expression of "we're all in this together."

---

[5] Danny Meyer, *Setting the Table: The Transforming Power of Hospitality in Business* (Harper Collins, 2006).

That sentiment is more than the refrain from the High School Musical blockbuster or a mere platitude used in TV commercials during COVID-19 to encourage collectivist thinking. It is most often born from relationships, real ones, where you truly know another person and, as a result, have a stake in both their individual experience and your common experience as members of the same community.

In the best schools everyone also feels that they have a stake in the desired outcome: student achievement. They view themselves as part of a distributed leadership model, each responsible for a specific, integral piece. They are deeply motivated to execute their specific piece with excellence and to help others do the same.

"Engagement" includes specific steps that schools can take to maximize the chances that people will share their gifts, across their individual circles of influence and in a rigorous way. This is how cultures grow and are perpetually renewed.

"Engagement" lays out the case for why the choices made by leaders, even for the most routine sort of initiatives, can never be random. If every choice is not aligned with explicit reference to the vision and the people entrusted with delivering it, the impact can never be more than middling.

When leaders are active managers in building engagement, they harness the organization's most powerful resource: the hearts and minds of its people. It yields the potential to transform lives—the lives of students, the lives of families, and the lives of staff.

Part 3, "Execution," is the most tactical portion of *All In*. It describes the lessons we have learned from experience and from the examples of other organizations in how to be intentional in making a vision visible in everything a school does. It ensures that our choices in execution do not unintentionally undermine the very thing we set out to do.

A classic pitfall when we encounter a challenge to realizing our vision is to jump straight to solutions. Even when there is not a challenge but simply the spark of a new idea, we often fast-track to the execution phase. We are well-intentioned in our aspiration to move quickly toward outcomes that will better the organization and its people. The risk is that we fail to properly assess whether the gap is truly in execution or might instead be resulting from lack of clarity in our vision or lack of engagement among our stakeholders. Every decision in the realm of execution must be aligned in service of the vision and alongside engaged stakeholders who will be entrusted with execution.

Another pitfall readers should be wary of is the tendency to read terminology in this book and automatically think, "Great, we do that!" Be cognizant of this reaction; many of the concepts and methods described in this book are, by themselves, rather ordinary. What is not ordinary, and what sets organizations with strong, beneficial, and sustained cultures apart, is the intentionality behind their planning and execution of these concepts and methods. In other words, if you find you are patting yourself on the back for giving swag or spending money on high performers without thinking deeply about whether that swag or money have the intended impact (i.e., whether they serve your vision), then you are doing yourself and your school, and this book, a disservice.

With those preconditions satisfied, our focus can properly shift to execution. How we attend to the before, during, and after phases of any initiative will ultimately determine its impact. A great idea reinforced solely through wishful thinking won't hit. How we allocate the finite resources of time and treasure and what we choose to recognize (or not) will serve to either reinforce our vision or to undermine it. And how we endeavor to continually court both the talent that is central to fulfilling our vision and the talent that is the purpose for the vision will determine whether we have a school program to deliver at all.

The crucial thing to remember is that culture is not a silver bullet that can fix an ineffective school model. A school can follow all the steps described in *All In*, but they will be for nothing without an effective model, including, for example, strong curriculum, operations, and budget management. That's on you. Conversely, and what schools throughout the country are now realizing, even the strongest school model can fail if not fueled by an equally strong school culture. That's where we can help.

The "Why" of Culture

There is an often-told story about President John F. Kennedy's visit to Cape Canaveral during the Apollo program. Kennedy asked a man mopping the floor what his job was.

"Mr. President, I'm helping to put an astronaut on the moon," the man replied.

That was the feeling we intended for everyone at Brilla when we launched in September 2013. Like the Apollo program, we would build a culture in which every member was integral to the realization of our vision to educate and support the holistic development of our students, in order for them to flourish. We intended a clear through line from our vision to engagement and execution.

"Intention" and "intentional" are words you will read a lot in this book. At Brilla we talk all the time—out loud—about being intentional in the choices we make. Saying out loud what we have all signed up for—and holding ourselves accountable to it—is characteristic of our culture.

Why be intentional about culture? That custodian at NASA was getting a paycheck, right? What did it matter how he viewed his job as long as the job was done? Why worry at all about his level of commitment to the organizational vision, about whether he felt like part of the community? Why care if he was all in?

More so than in other fields, education happens through people. All fields have a human element, but in ours people directly teach and motivate people through their hearts and minds. This is accomplished through staff, both in classrooms and in offices; through families, who are a child's first and greatest introduction to love and learning; and through students, the protagonists of their educational journey.

Our intention is that every role in the organization is not just going to be respected. Our intention is that everyone—students, families, staff—is integral to fulfilling our vision.

We work every day to get students, families, and staff bought into the vision and bought into each other. There is a difference between doing work because you have to and doing work because you feel called to, on both a rational and emotional level. It makes all the difference to outcomes, especially on the dark days. And there will always be dark days.

Never was that more evident than during the COVID-19 pandemic. Why did teachers, staff, students, and families all commit to showing up in person when doing so might put their lives at risk? We were one of the only charter schools in New York City to return to in-person teaching in the fall of 2020. Why did our teachers, staff, students, and families remain committed to Brilla when they had options to join other fully remote schools?

Because there was trust and commitment, in both the vision and each other, and Brilla's culture (carefully cultivated in service of that vision) served both as a bond and self-motivating force during this trying time.

Culture is not just one thing. Culture is the sum of many intentional practices. We—all of us, whatever our jobs—need to feel commitment to a clearly expressed vision if we are to align our energies and collaborate toward its realization. In a people-driven industry, commitment correlates directly with results. Leaders facilitate that sense of commitment. There is a definable method of culture building. It rests on the great insight that no one can be compelled to do anything of lasting value.

Culture is a multilayered concept.

Culture is not one-dimensional. It is not simply trying to make your employees happy. It is not as simple as amenities in a break room or a fun outing after the workday. If only it were!

When I was appointed as culture lead in my first teaching job, a lot of my colleagues thought of the role as a kind of minister of fun. For the record, I am in favor of fun (I have been described by a friend as a "fun evangelist" and by colleagues as the "queen of joy"). In fact, part of my founding role as director of community and culture involved inculcating an intentional culture of joy, which may be why some colleagues still tend to confound the broader concept of culture with joy and retain a myopic view of culture. But they are not the same. Joy, or positive morale, is often an outcome of strong culture, because membership in a community united by common purpose often yields positive feelings. But culture encapsulates a broader concept that can be applied across all kinds of visions.

Not long ago I led a training session for charter school leaders. Afterward I was approached by a principal who described his vision of a school that stressed service to members of the school community and to the world at large. I thought that was a cool idea. "But don't do anything just because it is a cool idea," I urged him. "Do it with a vision of what your success looks like. Be able to say out loud what your vision is in a clear way that every single member of your organization can understand, repeat back, and live up to. That way it will shine through every choice you make at school. And," I added, "when it doesn't shine through, you'll know."

In other words, intentionally bake the vision into your school culture.

It was the sort of moment when you hear what comes out of your mouth and realize how utterly convinced you are that what you are saying is the truth.

Since opening our first school in 2013, any time we have introduced a new practice or a new perspective, we have challenged ourselves to consider whether it intentionally supports our vision for how we do school, and what intentional practices will be required to make it live as part of our culture.

For someone like the principal at the conference, the ideal core element of school culture might be framing education as a means to enrich the lives of others. A different school might posit the purpose of education as a means for achieving social justice and then craft every element of its culture aligned to that view. For a religious school it could mean imbuing the curriculum with the tenets of a theology. For other schools the culture might focus staff and students alike on achievement as the ultimate aim, likely evidenced through high test scores. What all these should have in common is an intentional and fully integrated culture that attracts the right talent aligned with a clearly expressed vision, and then nurtures that talent to promote the vision.

Culture is defined, in part, by a shared vision.

For the stakeholder groups in a school community, clarity of vision is prerequisite. Teachers cannot model for children externally what they are not devoted to internally. Families cannot be partners in furthering school-driven goals for their children if they do not share the commitment to those goals.

Brilla's view is that the purpose of education is the formation of children's intellect, character, and spirit. The ultimate outcome is a flourishing life. We want this for our staff and we want it for our families. Above everything, though, we want it for our students. These three elements form the basis for our particular school culture. They are baked into everything we do.

The ultimate aim of intentionally building organizational culture is to unite people across the school community, in small things and large things, in service of a shared vision.

It is safe to say that every school has a similar basic mission: the education of its students. There are some variations on that, of course. But at the core, the mission is a simply stated assertion of what you hope to achieve. Culture is the "how" of accomplishing the mission. Culture, as we use the term in this book, is more than just the vibe you get when you walk into a school building. It also transcends the work that goes into creating that feeling—structuring the school schedule, defining the curriculum, programming events, building the organization chart and so on. It's all of those things and more.

The pitfall into which so many schools fall is that leadership goes straight to the work of devising the execution-based elements of their school program without taking time to unpack their mission into a robust vision, which is the guiding "how we do school" that informs every subsequent action and makes culture come to life.

Two different schools, for example, might both claim character development for students as part of their mission. One might do it by holding up great exemplars of character, defining why character matters, and providing opportunities for students to grow in character by allowing them to make mistakes. The other might implement a rigid reward-and-consequence system as a means for teaching right and wrong. Though the missions are the same, the visions for how are quite different. The vision for how, more so than the mission of what, will inform the development of school culture.

Even if you successfully develop a vision, another common pitfall is adopting practices without considering how, or even if, they support the school's vision. A common thing in some charter schools, for example, is so-called silent breakfast, in which kids are expected to start their day reading quietly. For some schools that might serve the mission and reflect the vision. At Brilla we start each morning with a mini pep rally called "Bird Call." (Our mascot is, after all, a big, bright red cardinal. More about that later.) It is a cultural ritual that energizes the whole building as we start the day. Why? Because promoting a strong sense of community is one aspect of our vision. Breakfast is one of the few times each day when the whole school community is physically together. For us, implementing silent breakfast would be a missed opportunity to further our vision.

To develop strong culture, a vision must be more than a school's mission statement. Vision should be expressed in all organizational processes, from daily interactions with kids and families to the ways staff connect with each other in the break room. These coalesce into culture.

Culture is inevitable.

Whether planned or not, organizations will inevitably develop a culture. Amy Radin, an expert on managing business innovation,[1] has observed that in most organizations culture is just something that happens. There is no intentionality.

"Bad culture," Radin has said, "is like mildew. It's awfully hard to get rid of."

Whether we intend it or not, culture will be born; a way of "doing things around here" will emerge. It will either be inspired by a mission-driven vision to inform the "how," or it will emerge organically, often from random sources: perhaps a dominant group of staff members breed it; it may be carried over from people's experience in their previous place of work; it may result as an extension of how people carry on when they are at home. Crossing our fingers and hoping a strong culture will magically realize itself will never be enough. When we do not act with intention, we get a culture that reflects that lack of intentionality. Culture aligned to a vision will have a positive net effect.

---

[1] Amy Radin, *The Change Maker's Playbook* (City Point Press, 2018).

Culture misaligned to a vision will have a negative net effect. There is no net neutral.

Culture impacts outcomes.

A commonly expressed piece of conventional wisdom is that smart organizations hire good people and then leave them alone to do their jobs. There is an obvious passivity in that outlook. It suggests that outcomes are disconnected from the reasons why people work and minimizes the extent to which outcomes are influenced by the organizational structures that shape every interaction people have within an organization, even the smallest. This would be the same as saying that in a school context a teacher's strong instructional methods are enough to ensure the desired outcome of student learning, without regard to the lesson plan quality or classroom dynamics.

This conventional wisdom is wrong.

A 2021 survey by the Society for Human Resource Management (SHRM) found that 97 percent of senior executives believe their actions have a direct effect on workplace culture. Among human resources professionals, 52 percent spend at least ten hours a week managing employee culture. Some spend twice that much time.

Among employees surveyed by SHRM, 53 percent say they have left a job because of workplace culture.[2] In an era of labor shortages, there is an almost unprecedented willingness to quit an unfulfilling job.[3] Especially in our pandemic-influenced society, the evidence has never been stronger that culture impacts outcomes. If teachers don't show up, students won't learn. If families don't send their students to school, they won't learn. Even if the teachers and the students do show up but only put forth the bare minimum amount of effort, learning will

[2] "The Culture Effect: Why a Positive Workplace Culture Is the New Currency," Society for Human Resource Management, September 2021.

[3] Juliana Kaplan, "The Psychologist Who Coined the Phrase 'Great Resignation' Reveals How He Saw It Coming and Where He Sees It Going. 'Who We Are As an Employee and As a Worker Is Very Central to Who We Are,'" *Business Insider*, October 2, 2021.

be limited. In contrast, if both are deeply invested in one another and the shared outcomes to which they aspire, learning will multiply.

Culture is the work of leaders.

Because culture is crucial to outcomes, leaders must be accountable to it.

In an extensively researched article for *Harvard Business Review*, Boris Groysberg and his colleagues concluded that "executives are often confounded by culture because much of it is anchored in unspoken behaviors, mindsets, and social patterns. Many leaders either let culture go unmanaged or relegate it to HR, where it becomes a secondary concern for the business. This is a mistake, because properly managed culture can help them achieve change and build organizations that will thrive in even the most trying times."[4]

Building a productive culture can be pursued with the same rigor with which we pursue any other strategic objective. And it is a leader's responsibility to do it.

The highly influential DiSC personal assessment tool is used by more than a million people every year to improve teamwork, communication, and productivity. It categorizes the work of leaders under the headings of:

- Vision: an organization's imagined future state.
- Alignment: the work of winning support for the vision from everyone who will have a role in making it a reality.
- Execution: making the future state real by putting the right conditions in place.[5]

---

[4] Groysberg et al., "The Leader's Guide to Corporate Culture," *Harvard Business Review,* January–February 2018.

[5] For a case study of applying DiSC to organizational development, see Matthew J. Painter and Jean Ann Larson, "Case Study: Designing HIPO Programs That Work," *Chief Learning Officer,* August 10, 2021.

A leader's greatest power resides in the capacity to set a vision and to bring people together in engaging that vision and marshaling resources in execution of the vision.

Applying these principles, leading strong culture should be as concrete an objective on a leader's list of goals as the more specific goals of, for example, improving student achievement, reducing staff turnover, improving school safety, or increasing parent satisfaction. What's more, cultivating an intentional culture has the potential to positively impact all of those other specific goals. It is central to any leader's job. Despite the complex interpersonal dynamic presented by this particular goal, we can be methodical in how we accomplish it.

Culture relies on influence.

When managed with intention, a culture is something everyone in the organization can describe and use as a guide in making choices. In their book *Humanocracy*[6] Gary Hamel and Michele Zanini remark that "we need to put human beings, not structures, processes, or methods, at the center of our organizations. Instead of a management model that seeks to maximize control for the sake of organizational efficiency, we need one that seeks to maximize contribution for the sake of impact." If a feeling of universal participation is so critical to impact in organizations, why isn't it a hotter topic in management circles? Probably because people are complex, certainly more so than numbers on a spreadsheet or other key drivers of outcomes that can be more easily manipulated.

And here is the enduring truth of working through people: you cannot force anyone do anything. If a teacher, for instance, simply shouts at a student to stop having side conversations while instruction is going on, will the student necessarily stop? If the teacher threatens a consequence, is it guaranteed to work? If a teacher is receiving a

---

[6] Gary Hamel and Michele Zanini, Humanocracy: Creating Organizations as Amazing as the People Inside Them (*Harvard Business Review* Press, 2020).

paycheck, will that alone be enough to inspire them to analyze student work rather than merely grade it? Because families are expected to attend family conferences, will they come?

As leaders of a classroom, of a grade team, of a campus, indeed of any kind of organization, we may have formal power to command our teams. But the power of command is a lot less than we imagine.

In the summer before we launched in 2013, our founding team attended a "Teaching with Love and Logic" training session. The Love and Logic methodology[7] is rooted in a philosophy of childhood development established in the 1970s by psychiatrist Foster Cline in collaboration with a pair of educators: Jim Fay, a school administrator; and Charles Fay, a school psychologist. (Among other things, the trio coined the term "helicopter parent.")

The Love and Logic model begins with controlling the emotions of the adults in charge of children, not the other way around. It puts the stress on empathy when teaching consequences and establishing boundaries. It champions empowerment rather than control.

What appealed to our founding team about Love and Logic was that it supported our conviction, born of experience, that culture, any kind of culture, good or bad, is all about influence. Leaders in any setting cannot compel anyone do anything, certainly not anything in which people will fully invest themselves. Compulsion may win compliance but never commitment. Commitment is core to culture, and earning it is hard work.

Influence comes from many sources.

One expression of organizational culture is the structure of its systems and processes. What gets rewarded? What gets punished? Those structures influence behavior. In a strong culture everyone models the culture for everyone else. So socially, the other members of the school

---

[7] See, for instance, Jim Fay and Charles Fay, *Teaching with Love and Logic: Taking Control of the Classroom*, (Love and Logic Institute, 2016).

community also influence behavior. Finally, an individual's sense of drive and abilities influence their behavior. The more sources of influence at play, the better the odds for success in influencing behavior. This is what we have learned to call the influencer model.

The idea of modeling the influences at play in an organization is one Brilla adapted from *Influencer: The New Science of Leading Change.*[8] The influencer model may not have shaped the founding of Brilla, but it has been essential reading in reinforcing our culture and accomplishing our mission. We use the model as a tool to ensure we are being strategic in the way we leverage the different sources of influence to motivate behaviors that will help realize our vision.

Consider, for instance, what the influencer model categorizes in the table below as structural motivation: rewards and consequences. This powerful source of influence can be designed to motivate intended behaviors and shape the culture. Brilla has applied this method successfully by offering incentives to students who meet their individual performance goals on the nationally normed NWEA MAP tests that assess math and literacy achievement. We have used it to reward teachers who demonstrate mastery of their craft by inviting them to join a master teacher cohort that provides advanced developmental opportunities, such as attendance at external conferences, as well as a generous stipend.

However, again, this tool—like any of the methods in this book—must be implemented thoughtfully. If, for example, rewards and consequences are implemented without thought for how they support your vision, they may have unintended consequences that ultimately demotivate the desired behaviors.

---

[8] Joseph Grenny et al., Influencer: The New Science of Leading Change, 2nd ed. (McGraw-Hill Professional, 2013).

	Motivation	**Ability**
Personal	Make the undesirable desirable	Teach them to do what they can't
Social	Harness peer pressure to provide encouragement	Find strength in numbers to provide assistance
Structural	Design rewards and demand accountability	Change the environment

Source: Grenny et al., Influencer.

For example, we once had the excellent idea of establishing a competition to motivate higher achievement on a reading exam. The class that earned the best scores overall would be declared the winner and earn a prize in the form of an excessively large trophy. It worked, insomuch as the winning class saw their outcomes soar. Yet interestingly, overall achievement for the grade as a whole dropped. We realized later that the structural motivation was not encouraging collaboration but was instead encouraging competition among the teachers of different classes. If my class is rewarded for getting the highest grades, then I am demotivated to help your class get higher grades. Teachers were literally harboring resources—one of the low points in the evolution of Brilla's culture. The specific reward structure of pitting class against class promoted a zero-sum mindset and yielded a consequence worse than if there had been no reward at all.

To reiterate, this example is not meant as a knock against the use of structural motivation. It is meant to illustrate the importance of applying the model intentionally, in a manner aligned with the goals of your culture (in our case, teacher collaboration). Leaders mess this up all the time.

For another example, think about what the influencer model refers to as structural ability—the capacity for action that organizational structures enable. If Brilla wants teachers in a grade to be collaborators but we do not build shared prep time into their teaching schedule, then when can they be expected to collaborate during the day? This structural oversight would actively discourage the behaviors we want.

Thinking in terms of influencers gives an enormous boost to intentionality in shaping a vision-driven culture. People in our school community shine brightest and deliver the strongest outcomes when they are given the capacity to become engaged by drawing on both their motivations and abilities. Leaders can harness these methods to influence members of the community to act in ways that support the goals expressed in the organizational vision.

Sometimes it can feel like a lot to ask a school community to be *all in*, and to put the pieces in place to help them get there. Important work always asks a lot. What sustains high performance is commitment to the vision and our sense of connection to one another. Culture is a reinforcement of both.

But it doesn't have to be a mystical practice. There are concrete steps you can take. I will walk you through them in the chapters that follow.

PART 1

VISION

Dream In Detail

In the late 1940s Walt Disney had a vision for an amusement park—hardly a novel idea, even at that time. Amusement parks had the same mission then that they do now: entertainment and the separation of parents from their money. Disney had a vision of something else altogether.

In traditional parks, parents were passive spectators of their children. Disney dreamed of parents and children playing together and drawing closer, sharing their delight. In 1948, Walt wrote a memo to a Disney production designer detailing a fully formed vision for a Disney amusement park. This was not a one-page overview. It described vividly the details he envisioned for the park, details that exist to this day. Those details included incredibly specific descriptions of the main village of what would become the Magic Kingdom, including the iconic railroad station, the surrounding village green, the town hall (and its façade and the administrative building hidden within), the location of park benches, the bandstand, drinking fountains, trees, and shrubs. According to Walt's memo, "It will be a place for people to sit and rest; mothers and grandmothers can watch over small children at play. I want it to be very relaxing, cool, and inviting."[1] Walt's vision did not stop with the main village; it included detailed descriptions of Disney-themed carnival rides, a Wild West frontier town, a scale model steam-powered train to take guests to and from the park, Disney-themed shops, and the details of the futuristic Tomorrowland.

This vision informed everything about the design of Disneyland when it opened in 1955.

It was a vision so convincing and so clearly expressed that it did not depend on one person to make it come to life. When Disney died in 1966 his successors knew exactly what he would have wanted Walt Disney World to be when it opened in Florida in 1971. Since then the company has added additional "campuses" around the world, all of them adapted to their location but still manifesting the power of the founding vision.

I am telling you about Disney because it is a powerful example of what dreaming in detail can do for hearts, minds, and outcomes.

Brilla also started with a vision that needed to be dreamed in detail. Like the original Disneyland, it had a familiar mission, in our case the education of children. Less familiar was the nuance of offering access to a free, high-quality, holistic education to families in underresourced communities. So we undertook to dream in detail about how we would accomplish this vision.

To capture the full scope of Brilla's vision and the way we have dreamed it in detail would require a separate book. As a matter of fact, we have written that book, which we call *Essential Practices* and which we use internally every day. It describes in Brilla-specific ways

---

[1] Michael Broggie, *Walt Disney's Railroad Story: The Small-Scale Fascination That Led to a Full-Scale Kingdom* (Donning, 2006), 88.

how we design our school to help students experience beauty in a piece of music, marvel at the concept of symmetry in both a math problem and in the world around them, or connect with a storybook character in a way that inspires them to live more virtuously. It describes the ways in which we shape the experience of our staff so that they feel integral, effective, empowered, and fulfilled. It describes how we engage families, our partners, to uplift them as the first educators of their children as we undertake this journey together. And it describes how we pursue these aims with a great deal of intentionality, an undercurrent of joy, and efforts to cultivate a welcoming community, so that we can all flourish.

We started with a mission to help form students who are academically capable and virtuous, and then dreamed up a vision for all the conditions that would need to be in place to make that mission live. But if you come away from this chapter saying to yourself, "They want me to replicate what they do at Brilla," then you will have missed the point.

The point is that, just as it was for Walt Disney, having a stated mission is not enough. Having a clear vision for how we will fulfill that mission is indispensable to the creation of a great school. This is nonnegotiable. Then comes the work of dreaming in detail every dimension of your school program that will bring that vision to life—lesson plans, talent management, communications, budgeting, architecture...everything. Every detail in every choice you make should be informed by your intentions for the realization of your vision. It is your path to achieving the mission.

....

HERE IS WHAT YOU ARE SIGNING UP FOR IN THIS CHAPTER:

* **Start with your "what."** Create a clear, accessible, and universal headline that tells the world what you want your organization to become.
* **Explain your "why."** Describe the core beliefs that lead you to prioritize that specific element of your school vision.

* **Unpack your big idea.** Brainstorm—dream in detail—what it would look like for vision to be core to your program and how to make that happen. Involve all stakeholders in this effort. A great vision is nothing without specific ways to promote that vision.

* **Get descriptive.** You probably already have an idea in your head of what your concept will look like once it is up and moving in the world. Be as specific as you can be about the methods for promoting your vision and, again, do it as part of a team of stakeholders.

* **Get sensory.** Investment in a great cause rises dramatically when our connection to it reaches us viscerally. Enlist all five senses in clarifying the details of your vision.

* **Apply the vision to all stakeholders.** For the whole to cohere, you need to build conviction into all the places where the organization touches its members.

* **Measure your success.** Determine both qualitatively and quantitatively what success will look like. Articulate how you will know when you have nailed it.

Start with your "what."

Complete this sentence: "I want my school to be..." Your answer is where you start the work of dreaming in detail.

A compelling vision is clear, accessible, and universally understood inside and outside of your immediate community. It might be academic achievement, social justice, scientific innovation, environmental awareness, the infusion of traditional education with religious precepts, or any number of other big things. Whatever it is, you need to name it plainly. It may even be drawn directly from your mission statement.

Before Brilla's doors opened in 2013 we had clarity on our "what." We wanted our school to offer free, high-quality, holistic education for students in underresourced communities, inspired by three key elements: classical education, character formation, and joy. That was our "what." That was our starting place. (For the purposes of describing what it means to dream in detail, I will focus in this chapter on just one element: character formation.)

Explain your "why."

Just as we needed to be able to name the "what" of our vision, we needed to be able to communicate its "why" before we could start dreaming in detail. If you start organization building before you know your "why," you run the risk of instituting cultural practices unrelated to, and in some cases in opposition to, the realization of your vision.

For example, in too many instances "character" in a school setting is treated as a euphemism for disciplined behavior—compliant kids, silent hallways. Our vision of character formation is holistic, inclusive, and far-reaching. In Brilla's case, once we were able to explain the character portion of our vision, we could begin to detail a deliberate set of conditions, practices, and encounters to ensure children could regularly access their internal goodness and virtue and recognize that same goodness and virtue in the world around them.

We intended that Brilla students would learn to do the right thing because it was the right thing, because a virtuous life is the highest pursuit. We intended to structure an environment that leverages the logic of the natural rewards and consequences of living in society. If we wanted students to be good, then we should be teaching them not simply to seek reward or avoid a negative consequence but to be virtuous because of the impact their choices have on themselves and others.

Once we could explain the "why" of the character portion of our vision, we could begin dreaming up practices to support a school that uplifted character as a core element, one where students, families, and staff came together in pursuit of a virtuous life and an educated mind. The "why" of this core element of our vision produced cascading effects on our practice. It has never stopped rippling across our school organization, even as we expanded to five campuses.

Unpack your big idea.

At the lowest point of the 2020 COVID-19 crisis David Brooks, the conservative political commentator, remarked that the president was "unlettered. He has no literary, spiritual or historical resources to draw upon in a crisis." The great leaders Brooks admired "were educated under a curriculum that put character formation at the absolute center of education. They were trained by people who assumed that life would throw up hard and unexpected tests, and it was the job of a school, as one headmaster put it, to produce young people who would be 'acceptable at a dance, invaluable in a shipwreck.'"[2]

We dreamed of a school that would produce just such individuals. But how?

Putting character formation "at the absolute center of education," in Brooks's phrase, is a defining characteristic of a "classical" education, one in which students are explicitly taught virtue. In fact, the objectives of a classical education are derived from Aristotle's four cardinal virtues (as adapted by Brilla to promote comprehension by young students):

Wisdom, or making thoughtful choices demonstrated in word and action with knowledge of the things that matter.

Self-control, or actively monitoring voice and body by considering their impact and exercising power over impulses.

Courage, or doing what is right in the face of fear and finding the strength to persevere, and having a willingness to venture when unsure.

Justice, or fairness. Giving to each what is due, consistent with one's dignity.

Aristotle believed that a fully formed character exhibited all four of these virtues. An Aristotelian character—the pursuit of a "complete life," as he called it—was a prize aspiration of Brilla's vision from its beginnings. It is embodied in each of the five attributes of a Brilla scholar: dignified, classical, expert, balanced, and relational.

---

[2] David Brooks, "If We Had a Real Leader," *New York Times*, May 28, 2020.

Unpacking this element of our vision and beginning to make it live in our school started with communicating it among our staff. We would then cascade it to our students and families.

Of note, despite character being a core element of our mission statement from our founding, we did not take the time to dream in detail a vision for how to bring it to life during year one. The lack of intentionality showed in our early years: a kindergartener once asserted that the action of his pencil soaring across the room was due to a lack of self-control on the part of the pencil—evidence that it's never too late to get started.

In year three, we recognized the opportunity we were missing and invited Jolleen Wagner to join our team to lead this visionary work. She was Brilla's first character initiatives lead. The depth of our approach is a testament to her ability to dream in detail about this critical component of our school design. And yet, Jolleen also recognized that for a vision to take root, we needed to facilitate a feeling of shared ownership over this thing we were designing. We asked the staff to brainstorm what it would look like for character to be core to our school program. We asked families, too. Already we understood that dreaming in detail was something that could not be done alone in an office by just a few members of the leadership team.

Get descriptive.

One thing became immediately clear as we unpacked our idea for Brilla's focus on character: if we really believed in the pursuit of what Aristotle called a "complete life," then we would have to dream in detail about how to teach our kids to grow in virtue all through the school day. Relegating character formation to a stand-alone instructional block would be inconsistent with our belief that growing in character can and should be an ongoing pursuit.

We would still need a dedicated block of time to introduce a virtue concept, but then we would need to build opportunities to reinforce it. These could come in additional structured school day blocks, such as a check-in during the middle of the school day and an opportunity to reflect at its end. But we could also ensure that the concept of virtue would be reinforced by building it into lessons from other subject areas and using virtue language when encouraging or correcting student behaviors, the ways staff engaged one another, and more. This is what we mean by "get descriptive"—it's the answer to the question "What do you mean when you say character development should be ongoing throughout the day?"

Just as a good teacher might seize on a history lesson to reinforce a math concept, they can also seize on an academic lesson to reinforce virtue. These opportunities can even be cued up beforehand in a lesson plan. If the class is reading about Robin Hood, for example, that is a good opportunity to discuss concepts related to virtue, and how Robin demonstrates them (or not). But what about the unplanned moments in the course of a day? We needed to dream about how to incorporate explicit and implicit opportunities to help students develop virtue knowledge and understanding.

Say a student makes a bad choice in class. Maybe he calls out without raising his hand. In a traditional rewards-and-consequences model, his teacher would give him a demerit or say, "OK, get up and turn your card to red." There would be little reflection at all about the "why" behind the consequence. The vision of growing in virtue would be undermined.

Instead, the teacher might ask, "What is the impact on everyone else if you call out? Why should you hold yourself back from calling out the answer?" The change in tactics derives from the desire to see an incremental growth in virtue. Just as we can grow in our knowledge of history, we can grow in virtue when we create and recognize deliberate supports to make it happen.

I've elaborated upon just one element of our vision for character by responding to the prompt "What do you mean when you say character development should be ongoing throughout the day?" But you can, and should, dream in even further detail by posing that essential question—"What do you mean by X?"—for every piece of your answer to this prompt. For example, if you are trying to answer what it means to develop character throughout the day, you should ask, and answer, questions about what it means to reflect at the end of the day. "What does it mean to use virtue language when encouraging or correcting student behaviors?" "What exactly is virtue language, and what would it sound like?"

The more detailed the description and the richer and more resonant the vision, the easier it will be to make decisions in service of it and get people invested.

Get sensory.

The next level of dreaming in detail is to go beyond words and find ways to make the description visceral. Literally, get sensory.

Hear it.

Something any teacher knows for a fact is that the kids are always listening (sometimes when we wish they weren't). So we dreamed about what it would sound like to be in a school where character is at the core.

Starting with basics, we would expect to hear polite phrases such as "please" and "thank you," kind words of greeting as people are welcomed to the school building, tones of voice that convey respect and honor dignity. Anything to the contrary would seem inconsistent with a school vision that uplifts character. But again, we can challenge ourselves to get richer in our details.

Essential to the way we teach students to grow in virtue at Brilla is in the use of what we call virtue language. Instead of "Don't give up," it's "I know you can seize this opportunity to show perseverance." In the example from the previous section, one step further than "Why should you hold yourself back from calling out the answer? What is the impact on everyone else if you call out?" would be to also leverage the virtue language of self-control. When students hear teachers using this language, they understand that attention is being directed to the character issues at stake in whatever is being discussed. The narration becomes less about the specific situation and more about the transferable takeaway.

In our next chapter—"Say What They Are Signing Up For," Step 2 of *All In*—we get granular about strategic communication that moves people to enlist in support of a great vision. Precise, inspiring language is indispensable to winning hearts and minds, as it is to the inspiration of high performance.

But by itself language is not enough. Kids and adults alike notice gaps between what we say and what they see.

See it.

The next sense to engage in describing your vision is sight. We asked ourselves, "What would we expect to see in a school that prioritizes character?"

We started with the obvious: visuals on the walls. If character is core, we would see photo exemplars of people who have modeled virtue. And those would not just be arbitrarily added to a bulletin board; they would be directly taught and discussed (connecting to our vision of a classical school). Photos of students who exemplify virtues would be displayed as well (connecting to our vision of a joyful school community). We would see our virtues displayed and defined, to reinforce everyone's understanding of what Brilla means by courage, dignity, and self-control.

Beyond visuals, we consider what we would expect to see in people's actions. Holding the door for the person behind you to demonstrate kindness, picking up a piece of trash that may not be yours to demonstrate respect for the physical environment of the school, running copies on the copy machine in reasonable quantities to demonstrate justice to your colleagues.

Again, we challenge ourselves to dream in greater detail by considering different contexts and situations. What would we expect to see in a classroom when two students have a disagreement, from the students involved, from the other students in the class, and from the teachers present? What would we expect to see when a family makes a complaint? When a staff member needs help in their classroom? When a lunch is put out for staff and quantities are limited?

Feel it.

Humans are reached in their deepest places through all five senses. I would add a sixth: emotion.

Every community—and schools are no exception—is attuned to how its members treat one another. If growing in character is an essential part of the vision, then our vision and our behavior had better match.

Say a staff member is running late to school, or a stranger comes in off the street. How should we react if we claim to value a fully formed character? Empathetically. If we are going to dream in detail about growing in virtue, we have to get empathy right.

Empathy is more than just kindness in the conventional sense. As an intentional practice, empathy is a tool of character formation. Empathy is recognizing that if a staff member is late, the reason is probably not that they do not respect Brilla's cultural value of punctuality. That is the rare person, and those people are likely to self-select out of the school because of a strong expectation of accountability from their peers. Our intention is for the culture to be exactly that strong.

If empathy is core to how we interact with children, then it had better be core to the way we treat adults, whether they are families or members of staff. It is not only kids living in underresourced communities who carry outside burdens to school every day, burdens that can limit access to their best selves. For a staff member it could be family problems, or a new baby who is keeping them up half the night. The ethos of most professionals when things go wrong is to put on their game face and just go to work. That is damaging not just to the person wearing the mask but also to the work they do.

A popular saying goes, "I have learned that people will forget what you said, people will forget what you did, but people will never forget how you made them feel." Sound and sight may be direct appeals to the core senses, but feelings go a step deeper to convey the sincerity of those words and actions, a topic we will take up in Step 6, "Accept All the Gifts."

Apply the vision to all stakeholders.

If every stakeholder in our organization does not believe deeply in the vision, none of what we envision will manifest in the culture. Conviction needs to be built into all the places where the organization touches its members—students, families, and staff.

Up to this point I have drawn mainly on the experiences of students and staff for illustrations of how we dreamed our vision in detail. But from the beginning we knew our model would depend on the full engagement of families as well. There is a great deal we learned from engaging families that turned out to be transferrable to our other stakeholders.

A core belief of Brilla schools is that families are the first educators, a child's first introduction to virtue and to love. We might be the ones to teach them geometry, but it would be preposterous to assert that we alone will teach them good character. Families will continue educating their children long after those children have left our school buildings.

You might say we have a business interest in winning the hearts and minds of families. The success of our vision is in fact dependent on the families who freely choose to enroll in our school. They must find our vision compelling enough to join as partners in the vision. We would be foolish not to have an unrelenting focus on family engagement.

This focus is sincere. Early on in the work of dreaming our vision in detail we settled on what in the business world is called a stretch goal. The goal was 100 percent attendance at family conferences. Anything less would be considered a failure.

There were lots of reasons given for why perfect attendance at family conferences was not a realistic goal. We were told that too many families did not care enough about their kids' education, that there were barriers to travel, lack of childcare, difficulty with scheduling jobs, and so on. If engaging families as full stakeholders was core to Brilla's vision, then we had to dream a way of overcoming these barriers.

We communicated our expectation clearly: every family was expected to attend family conferences, period. From that shared expectation we derived what we needed to do to make it happen, including identifying influencer strategies.

In some ways the family meetings stretch target was our first chance to apply techniques derived from the influencer model. We use influencer techniques to stimulate the personal motivation of families not merely to show up, but to understand how powerful it is to be a full partner in their child's education.

We provided families with what the influencer model would call personal ability. If, for example, families were shy about coming because there was a language barrier, we provided translators. We even offered a training session on what to expect at a report card conference. It was no good having conferences exclusively between five and seven thirty at night. Too many families were not home from work by then. So we provided early-morning and midafternoon conference hours as well.

What happened when, inevitably, a family did not show up for a conference at the school? We went to them. We went to their home; we went to their job. Some families were grateful for our persistence; others were annoyed. In either case, it signaled that we had a commitment to each other, a commitment all stakeholders had agreed to honor.

We have hit that goal every year, including on our new campuses. At last count, that's 1,400 families across five campuses. There is a shared pride in what 100 percent attendance says about our school community. Shared expectations create social motivation. Families hold one another accountable for keeping the attendance record perfect. They help each other: "I will pick up your kid so that you can come to school straight from work." We and they are creating different strategies to meet different family needs.

We cannot compel family involvement, which in any case would be counter to the Love and Logic philosophy. But we can intentionally create conditions to influence families and make it easier for them to be involved in the life of the school, backing up our core belief in the parent as first educator.

We saw pretty quickly that committed families are the most persuasive evangelists for our vision. So we dreamed in detail about how they could help realize our vision for character as well. We spotlighted elements of our character initiatives approach in family newsletters, for instance, and in our monthly Coffee and Conversations meetings, where we keep families up to date on what students are learning in the classroom. At these gatherings we share the virtue being focused on in school that month and ask what families are seeing at home. We train teachers to apply the virtue language referenced previously in everyday discussions with families, whether spontaneous or scheduled. Families are not only exposed to the core elements of our character initiatives approach, but they also help shape it. Some of our most impactful initiatives were inspired by families who participated in our annual listening circles.

Lessons we learned from one stakeholder experience proved to have application to other stakeholders. The actions we take in pursuit of our vision for character formation are not merely a manifestation of virtuous people behaving virtuously (though sometimes they are). Our organizational behaviors were—and are—also the product of intention.

All our teachers, for instance, keep journals describing their reflections on the virtues we hope to encourage in our students and deepen in ourselves. The journals capture their personal answers to the "why" of modeling and teaching virtue. Journal keeping primes teachers to seize teachable moments when they arise. Journals encourage greater empathy for what students experience as they develop in virtue by prompting teachers to reflect on what is, after all, an ongoing experience for all of us.

Teachers talk about their own growth in virtue the same way they talk about their growth in core knowledge and skills. "I used to have trouble showing this virtue," they might say, "but I have gotten better."

About once a month each Brilla school has a meeting in which staff members deeply reflect on one virtue, engaging with it in a personal way. We call them Mission in Progress meetings, or MIPs for short. MIPs are an intentional rebranding of the professional development concept adopted by many schools, which, let's be honest, often elicit eye rolls from staff. Our intention for MIPs is to extend development beyond pedagogy to all the elements that are core to our vision and culture—reading and math achievement, data analysis, social/emotional learning, actively participating in the school community, etc.

In MIPs focused on character formation, we might share reflections captured in our journals, insights developed from our daily lives as adults, or classroom experience about what virtue looks like for a second grader versus a seventh grader. Self-control, for instance, is a virtue that kids (and many adults) struggle with. We might talk about types of self-control and how a person may be strong in one type and weak in another. How would we strengthen the weak spot in ourselves? How can that reflection help us strengthen it in students?

It is an approach and a collection of insights that we can apply to all our stakeholders.

Measure your success.

Acknowledging that the work of dreaming in detail is never finished, what is your idea of what success will look like? How will you know when you've begun to nail it? What are your metrics?

For a vision to become real in the world, it needs metrics that tell us whether we are reaching our goal. These can be both qualitative and quantitative. How would Brilla, for example, know whether its concept of character is taking root apart from just encouraging students and teachers to think about virtue?

To a large degree the success of our program is evident—or not—when one walks into a classroom. Do the students exhibit virtue knowledge and understanding in all their lessons? Or do they do so only when it is explicit in the curriculum? Are teachers seizing unexpected opportunities for celebrating virtue? Do students demonstrate an understanding of good character in their relationships, not just with adults but with their peers?

Quantitatively, we assess whether the right inputs are in place, auditing whether both time and money are being allocated in support of this vision element at a given campus. (I discuss this further in Step 8, "Ledger Time and Treasure.") Our teacher evaluations have indicators to assess whether there is evidence that they are facilitating virtue formation for students.

Quantitatively measuring outputs for character is markedly more difficult, and something about which we routinely engage with other schools to learn best practices. Currently, our method is to survey parents, as they have the best eye for how their children display virtues across contexts. We make the survey more objective by asking parents to score observable traits that are grade-level appropriate, based on the frequency with which they observe them. As evidence of courage, does their child admit when they need help, were wrong, or made a mistake? For self-control, do they listen when others speak and refrain from interrupting? What we discover is a high correlation between what teachers notice in the classroom and what parents report.

We cannot prove causation—yet—but the correlation appears to be undeniable. I recall one student, for example, who was well known in our school community. In elementary school he struggled with the idea of courage and was uncomfortable speaking up. He feared being made fun of. But by middle school he had become remarkably comfortable with who he was and recognized his own value. Indeed, his mother relayed the story of how he spoke up in a group chat among friends when the kids began using profanity.

"We shouldn't be talking like this," he texted. That was the measure of a kid who had grown in virtue—just the way we dreamed it.

The lessons we have learned about the power of dreaming in detail—the power of discovering the "how" in our "what" and our "why"—can be applied in any organization. But even the most innovative vision will sputter if it is not communicated vividly in ways that make everyone feel as if they have signed up for something transformative. I address this subject in Step 2.

REFLECT ON YOUR PRACTICE

Start with your "what."
- What words or phrases are used to describe your organizational vision? Is there a universal headline that clearly communicates what you want your organization to become?

Explain your "why."
- What core beliefs are foundational to your vision?
- Which core beliefs might be difficult to teach and will require people to champion them intrinsically?

Unpack your big idea.
- How can your "what" be made more explicit or broken down into core tenets?
- What needs to be further elaborated?

Get descriptive.
- What details have you provided to help others understand what your vision actually looks like in practice? Be as specific as possible.

Get sensory.

- How can you leverage the five senses to make your vision visceral and tangible for all stakeholders? (Go through each sense: sight, hearing, smell, taste, and touch.)

Apply the vision to all stakeholders.

- How have you considered the application of your vision to each stakeholder group?

- What components of your vision are transferrable across stakeholder groups?

Measure your success.

- How will you know when your vision has been actualized?

- What combination of qualitative and quantitative data will you leverage to measure your progress and achievement?

Say What They Are Signing Up For

Taco Bell knows what it is: cheap and cheerful fast food. It is not a swank sit-down restaurant. It is not even Chipotle. Its market is anybody.

The Breitling watch company knows what it is: one of the fanciest makers of chronometers on Earth. You can spend $20 for a Timex or $5,000 for a Breitling. They have the same mission: both deliver timepieces that keep accurate time. The market for a Timex is anybody. The market for a Breitling is not; it is a decidedly more exclusive group of people willing and able to pay a premium price for a luxury watch.

What Taco Bell and Breitling have in common is that they know who they are and what they are about. This shows in all the ways they communicate about themselves. They get the details right. They repeat the same clear message again and again. Their customers know what they are signing up for.

Compared to these consumer brands, the communications strategies of too many organizations—schools especially—can feel ad hoc and unstructured. Care for precise language, clarity of intent, messaging consistency, concern for whether a message was received—none of it is pursued with rigor.

The measure of a successful communications strategy is that, if called upon, all stakeholders in an organization should be equipped to explain what they have signed up for. They should be able to tell a total stranger *how* the way things are done in their organization supports the vision. They should not need to refer to a handbook or kick the question up the line to someone who might explain it better.

In this chapter I describe the "how" of creating a communications strategy that ensures that everyone understands the vision, can describe why it matters, and can say why every action either supports it or does not.

Earning that kind of commitment, where stakeholders openly champion the vision at every turn, requires leaders to inspire a free choice to choose the school vision. For that to happen, stakeholders need to be hooked on the vision from day one, and on every day after. When that happens, they will be with you when times are great and when times are hard.

HERE IS WHAT YOU ARE SIGNING UP FOR IN THIS CHAPTER:

* **Be transparent.** This includes not only a habit of telling what you know but a habit of acknowledging what you may not know. Remember that respect begets respect, and that means being addressed with candor. It also means being apprised of change in advance of its arrival whenever possible.
* **Be clear.** Inspire your stakeholders by telling them what they get when they join your community. But do not overlook how inspiring it can be to tell your stakeholders how their contributions—what they must give—will make a vision come to life.

* **Be consistent.** Overcommunicate. Seize every opportunity to send your message. Express your vision as often as you can, beginning with your earliest contact with prospective stakeholders. Once you have built a track record for honesty, acquire a reputation for language that is unfussy, accessible, and direct.

* **Be effective.** Get in the habit of trying out your message with trusted audiences—cascading it—to absorb impact and make it more targeted. Worry over whether your messaging is sticking. Don't assume your message was received. You audience is bombarded with messages all day long. Cutting through the noise is one of the burdens of leadership.

Be transparent.

One of the most influential books among members of the Brilla team is the Jim Collins classic, *Good to Great: Why Some Companies Make the Leap...and Others Do Not.*[1] The subject of *Good to Great* is how good companies, mediocre companies, even bad companies can achieve lasting greatness—and why most fail to make the transition.

No chapter of *Good to Great* has proved more essential to us than the one titled "First Who...Then What." Collins employs a metaphor of a bus to illustrate the business—or, in our case, the school. He makes the case that having the right people on the bus makes it easier to change direction, minimizes the time required to motivate and manage people, and limits the potential for the wrong people to undermine the success of a great vision.

Defining the "who" among our stakeholders—kids, families, staff—has been a huge lever in developing our vision-driven school. The people come first. If we want the right "who"—students, families and staff—to choose to join us, then we are best served by being trans-

---

[1] Jim Collins, Good to Great: *Why Some Companies Make the Leap...and Others Do Not* (HarperBusiness, 2001).

parent about what they are signing up for—not just when they first come aboard, but again and again.

To be persuasive and win commitment, communications must be credible, professional, and respectful of your audience. Even before they come aboard, we communicate to students, families and staff— out loud, every day—that responsibility for creating a flourishing community belongs to all of us.

From the beginning we aim to set a tone of full transparency. For example, we tell everyone, and then we tell them again, that if they want a school where families drop off and pick up their kids without interaction, they will not like Brilla. We tell it to families; we tell it to staff even before they join us.

In a job interview for new staff, we might role play a student who repeatedly taps their pencil during instruction. It is not meant to be a gotcha moment. The purpose is to start a conversation about Brilla's vision for how a teacher might respond in a moment like this and to give both parties a chance to begin their relationship on a note of candor.

We hold that note for as long as the relationship endures. Once someone elects to join our school community, we continue communicating the vision at every opportunity.

Think of your audience when communicating the headlines of your vision. Worry about whether the language and media you use will appeal to them. Include the "why" behind each message, even the simple ones. Be as direct as you can be; don't embellish. Anticipate problems and misconceptions and address them head-on.

That is how great people expect to be addressed: with transparency.

Great people are so obviously central to the realization of a vision that, perversely, consistent communication with them can be forgotten. Too much gets taken for granted. There may be a mistaken assumption that everyone shares the same understanding of the vision. But time passes and focus may wander in the day-to-day swirl of all there is to do.

When times are uncertain, there can be a temptation to shave the truth. For a vision-driven institution that would be game over.

Say what you know.

During the COVID-19 pandemic I was reminded again and again of why transparency in communications is essential. At that most difficult moment in our school's history we were asking people to put themselves and even their families at risk just by coming to school.

In winning commitment to reopening we had to communicate that we honored freedom of choice among our stakeholders. We knew we were asking something big, and we acknowledged it. "We know that some of you have vulnerable loved ones at home, put at greater risk by your choice to report to school. We know that some of you feel forced to choose between personal safety and financial well-being. We know that re-envisioning school to be safely in person is a ton of effort that may all be for naught if we are unexpectedly required to go back to full remote." To do anything else would have been counterproductive and offensive. It would have betrayed the explicit promise of our vision.

We were clear about why reopening was essential to students and their families. We were consistent in delivering messages about expectations for the school year. We reopened, yes. More than that, everyone recommitted to the vision. A moment that might have broken the relationship with stakeholders instead became an opportunity for making it more solid.

Say what you don't know.

Throughout the COVID-19 epidemic we all felt frustration about how little anyone knew about the virus and its meaning for schools. Guidance changed almost daily. As school leaders we had to say what we knew and admit what we did not know. We did not set ourselves up as the coronavirus ministry of information.

When an organization is in crisis, it is too late to start thinking about a communication strategy. Trust that leadership is talking straight must be established beforehand. The structures of a rigorous communication strategy need to be already in place.

In any organization people respond well to being addressed with regard for their intellect. Most of us prefer to hear "we don't know yet" to hearing nothing at all or, even worse, happy talk.

Speak to the parts of your vision that are for the moment ambiguous. In an uncertain situation the correct strategy is to provide whatever details are available, even if it is only an expected timeline for when clarity will be reached, a process for how you plan to get to clarity, or an element in the vision that will guide your decision making.

Acknowledge change when you see it coming.

If change is coming, name it out loud when you see it coming. In this way you plant seeds so that your audience can mentally engage with change in advance of its arrival.

Being entrepreneurial brings with it the almost perpetual demands of change management. Any strategy consultant will tell you that. Sometimes this can make stakeholders feel like we have altered the terms of the deal they signed up for. That's because in some cases we have.

Context changes, inevitably. Strategies adapt. Communication strategies evolve. Even though we tried everything to clearly communicate our vision when we launched in 2013, for example, there have been things we learned along the way that caused us to adjust our approach.

For example, a core element in Brilla's mission is our expectation of consistently improving student performance outcomes. Brilla's first results from New York State standardized testing were not what we aspired to. We were not about to change this part of our mission, but we needed to adjust our vision for how we would realize it.

Inspired by Collins' metaphor, I gave an annual "on the bus" speech each year, in the spring right before staff members signed their renewal letters. I would share all the information I had about where the organization was headed in the next school year. The purpose was to activate their free choice, by reminding staff that in signing their renewal letters, they were choosing to recommit to Brilla's vision. It was a cue for them to reflect on whether they were still the right "who" for the work and if this was their bus. (The bus metaphor has since evolved to a train metaphor; more on that later.)

During this particular year, I told them that if they looked around the building and observed the colleagues they admired most, they would observe one particular trait in common: a reflex for solving problems rather than for simply pointing them out. "I want to be as transparent as I can," I said in that speech, "about what you are signing up for next year. Here's what's coming." And I told them. We lengthened the school day by half an hour. We did this because improving student performance outcomes was a core part of our relentless mission to help students succeed, and we believed that allowing more time for instruction during each school day would get us there. The decision affirmed our willingness to adapt elements of our vision when circumstances demanded it.

But we did not increase pay. Our finite budget for the next year was already accounted for, and an across-the-board raise was simply not feasible. That was hard; time has not diminished the deep disappointment of that moment. But we were as upfront as we could be with our staff about this change, despite the fact that doing so risked a staff exodus, which could have negatively impacted student achievement for entirely different reasons.

I reaffirmed our collective "why." "Our priorities remain the same," I said. "Everything we do is for our students. And we cannot in good faith look our families in the eye without feeling like we did everything we could to get their children back on track." And I acknowledged that that priority would be unachievable without staff buy-in. I explained that I understood the gravity of the change. And, ultimately, I gave them an opportunity to get off the bus if this restructuring was not for them.

We were sincere in wanting to make it OK for people to get off the bus if that was what they felt called to do. This was important for several reasons, not least because we had a couple of staff outliers who were not bought into the "why" behind the changes we were making. Behind closed doors they were chirping their discontent to the rest of staff. This was undermining the work we were doing to get things right. They had become the wrong "who" for our bus.

The peculiar thing was that these were good teachers. If skill was all that mattered, we would certainly have never let them go for cause. But they were toxic to the culture. In defense of the culture, we needed them to self-select out of Brilla (or implement a performance improvement plan). But it was best for both parties that we mutually acknowledged that the Brilla bus wasn't for them.

The solution lay in clearly communicating the adaptations to our vision. That made it clear to the naysayers that they would have been miserable staying while everyone else in the culture was rowing the other way. They chose to leave.

That year our retention rate was 74 percent—one of the lowest in our school's history. Yet, contextually, that's quite good for a NYC charter school, where average retention that year hovered around 60 percent.[2] I think the reason staff remained as committed as they did was because we communicated not just the "what" behind our change but its why. It was the "why" for which staff had enlisted in the first place, and the reason they stayed.

At that point we had only been around for a few years—we were literally a start-up. Before then we had not explicitly told ourselves that we were an entrepreneurial organization, and that therefore we needed to be flexible. It was the first time we said out loud that some things we sign up for will need to change if we see they are not working. Since then flexibility has become a defined expectation of our culture.

We say this out loud and as clearly as we can, all the time.

---

[2] Alyssa Katz, "Turnover, a Charter School Plague," *New York Daily News*, June 26, 2017.

Be clear.

Once you have committed to transparency you must clearly define the terms of what stakeholders give and what they get.

Say what they get.

First compel the audience with the benefits of membership. If they choose to sign up for this vision, what's in it for them? The message that should be embedded in every communication is this: do you want to be part of the best place possible for kids?

The information session we hold every winter is the first time families thinking of joining our community hear about our school in any detail and in a way that underscores the "why" of our culture. We tell them not only what they will get if they join Brilla, but also what we will ask them to give. If a family decides to join us, it is a message we will repeat over and over for the next nine years.

Even before a student has been admitted to school we are clear that we view family as the first educator. We make certain families know how seriously we take their central role in the education of their child. They are trusting us with their babies.

In any communication strategy analogies are powerful. With families we employ the analogy of unlocking your cell phone and handing it to a stranger. You had better be persuaded that you can trust the stranger. That is what parents do when they entrust their children to our school, though obviously the degree of responsibility we assume is incalculably greater.

We tell them this.

We tell families that their partnership in the Brilla vision is a centerpiece of our culture. We tell families that while we are not in the business of telling parents how to raise their kids, we are in the business of educating their kids. And we tell families very clearly and repeatedly that we want to—and the Brilla vision requires that we—do this work together.

In this way, families know what they are getting when they elect to send their children to Brilla. They understand that Brilla engagement does not end at the closing bell, and that Brilla will engage as a partner with families to best educate and help their children.

Say what they must give.

This level of family and student engagement cannot happen organically. It is facilitated by Brilla staff. And we clearly communicate to our staff what is expected of them. For example, it is a Brilla practice to issue cell phones to staff with the expectation that they will use them to return calls from families within one business day. Being on call this way is a big ask for staff. However, our staff members know—because they are told early and often—that honoring families as partners and first educators is core to our vision. So staff members know that the practice of being on call is anchored in that piece of the vision. It is what they signed up for.

If a staff member does not share the belief that allowing this kind of access from families is vital, then they are going to find our practice of being on call a burden. If it is not a good fit for them, honestly, that is OK. If you are clear from the get-go about what is being asked of staff, then they are offered the dignity of making an informed decision whether your organization is one they can buy into. In this environment, their free choice reinforces accountability to one another. For example, if a staff member questions why they are on call to families, others are likely to remind them that they signed up for exactly that (what the influencer model calls social motivation). Managed correctly it starts a wider conversation about expectations.

Our expectation is that everyone—staff, families, and students—participate in culture-building events. Our expectation is that everyone convey authentic welcome to families and total strangers. Our expectation is that we dress for work in ways that show we respect ourselves. Our expectation is 100 percent attendance at family conferences. Our expectation is that all of us model the commitment to growing in virtue.

We want staff galvanized by the vision and eager for a hand in realizing it. Above everything we tell staff we need educators who love children. And we do not use the word "love" casually.

Not all schools would say out loud that love is part of their expectation for an educator. "Love" for us means willing the good of the other. It is palpable throughout our school community, in the ways teachers welcome a visit and hug from a former student, and the way families invite teachers to important events like quinceañeras and christenings. It is evident in how we all inquire after each other beyond what is immediately applicable to the school setting, including celebrating the birth of a child or helping families that are suffering hardship. We want educators who sincerely embody that kind of love for children, as well as their families.

We are clear about this.

At multiple points throughout the year, from morning meetings to all-hands professional development sessions, we tell staff that our expectation is that they will model the qualities we hope to instill in our kids: joy, virtue, and a hunger for learning. We want them to show up each day for the right reason: for the children in front of them. We want them to make the children and their families feel prized. This is how our staff members show love.

We are clear about this.

Be consistent.

All through the school year we grab opportunities to repeat the expectations derived from our vision. Some are verbal, some are written, some are high impact and fully immersive. Some are planned, to ensure that the major points are reinforced during critical moments throughout the year. Others happen organically, when the opportunity to anchor an expectation in the vision presents itself. In morning meetings, in admissions celebrations, in family conferences, in restorative conversations with students, in written communications, when celebrating an employee of the month, or whenever students are in earshot of adult conversations—in all these rituals we seize the opportunity to reinforce what we have all signed up for.

Say it often.

Repetition is crucial to strategic communications. Still, insistence on talking about the vision can feel repetitive, especially for veterans among staff and families. But veterans are in many ways the most critical ambassadors for communicating the vision. They are the culture carriers. They are living proof that we mean what we say.

Just as every school experienced during the COVID-19 pandemic, members of our community tested positive for the virus. Understandably, staff and families wanted to know who tested positive just in case they may have come in contact with them. And we would not say, any more than we would broadcast which kid had head lice. If asked why, we pointed to a foundational element of our vision: to honor the dignity of the individual. Even if it was not the answer they wanted, we were seizing an opportunity to anchor our communications in the vision.

During an unprecedented event like COVID-19, the clarity with which we previously communicated expectations provided a foundation. Expectation of mutual accountability gave us language for talking about how every choice we made outside of school about masks and social distancing might impact the community we professed to love. We openly asked staff, students, and families to conduct themselves safely outside of school so as not to impact the school's ability to operate safely. If people chose to go another way, we did not condemn them. But we did ask them to reflect on whether their actions were consistent with the shared vision of our school community. We did it by appealing to the vision for which we were all signed up.

Instead of being a threat to our vision, the crisis became a chance to reaffirm it. We grabbed the opportunity.

Structure messaging so that it sticks.

Mark Twain once observed that the difference between the almost right word and the right word is the difference between the lightning bug and lightning. Twain might not have known the phrase "strategic communications," but he definitely knew the consequences of ideas communicated in a sloppy way.

Language that sticks is transparent, accessible, and direct. It might employ catchphrases or familiar analogies; it might be delivered by email, in a speech, or via a handout stuffed in a backpack. Just as it is for Taco Bell or Breitling, language that sticks must be consistent with the vision.

In a well-defined culture, expectations are transparent. Everyone is clear about what they signed up for. They know what they give; they know what they get. They hear it often. Take this one step further and capture these expectations in pithy language that resonates.

At Brilla we brainstormed how to better package messaging about core elements of our vision during a retreat in our fourth year. Our inspiration came from some troubling habits we saw emerging in our young organization that were counterproductive to our vision; for example, a staff member calling out sick for a week while posting vacation photos on social media. This inspired the Brilla norm "Honor the Team." On another occasion, a junior leader flipped the script during a team meeting by directing colleagues to clandestinely skirt organization-wide expectations with which she disagreed. This inspired the Brilla norm "Principle over Preference." We consciously reframed these incipient problems in ways that supported the aspirations of our vision. We have communicated them consistently ever since.

We were explicitly naming and explaining our norms. Norms should not be allowed to simply evolve until one day they are there, for better or worse. Naming them precisely is work. But it is work that pays dividends in reinforcing what we have all signed up for.

Be effective.

A Breitling, a Taco Bell, or any other organization that thinks hard about making its messages stick will test them with multiple audiences before they launch the campaign across their entire market. One name for this methodology is cascading.

Cascade with intention.

Picture two contrasting waterfalls, emanating from the same height. One rushes straight over the edge, directly from top to bottom. The impact when the water hits bottom is intense. There hasn't been anything to break up the force. The other flows over a sequence of falls. The force of impact is mitigated as it reaches the bottom, because each subsequent cascade has absorbed some impact. A message can be like that water. It can be tested on multiple groups, each one absorbing some of the impact and enabling you to learn from each communications experience to further refine and sharpen your approach.

For example, consider a principal transition. In a school as community oriented as ours is, this is a big deal. Imagine we were to simply share that announcement to all families and staff at the same time. The reaction would be intense. Those with the strongest personal views would likely set the tone for others. If some staff felt concern, families would notice that raw reaction.

Instead, we acknowledge that both stakeholder groups will have different concerns to address, so we convey the message in separate settings. We pilot the announcement with a smaller group of influential members who can help us anticipate the likely reaction and structure our messaging proactively.

Among families this means communicating first with members of the Family Involvement Committee, an elected group of parent leaders representing Brilla families' voice and perspective. We test our messaging to gauge how it hits. We also ask family leaders for feedback after they have had time to process the message. What will other families want to hear from us to inspire confidence in the transition? What concerns will be top of mind that we should transparently address head-on? Though this is done confidentially, in the event the communication is leaked the impact is still softened by allowing for private processing time.

For staff communications we follow a similar cascade by first communicating to staff leaders. The additional benefit is that when the message is ultimately cascaded to the wider staff, the leaders that other staffers look to will be able to convey a thoughtful position rather than raw emotion.

Everyone walks away knowing what they are signed up for in the next stage of the school's life. The initial impact of intense change is absorbed in a way that allows the school to stay focused on its essential work of implementing the vision.

Don't assume your message was received.

Just because something was communicated does not mean it was heard. And if it was not heard, we cannot immediately blame the audience. Imagine a teacher who told you it was not their fault that students did not learn a concept taught in their class. It would be laughable.

I will give you an example familiar to every school team.

Like all schools, sometimes Brilla is closed for a staff development day. We put this on the school calendar. We send flyers home. We make robotic phone calls. Still, some families don't get the message and come to school that day. It becomes a high-stress moment.

This breakdown in communication is not necessarily the fault of families. They are bombarded with messages from all directions in the course of a day, the same as all of us. We try to find rhythms in our routines, and anomalies may get missed.

Marketers know that messages get lost in the noise of our daily lives. That is why they are always dreaming up new ways to break through the noise that distracts all of us. When we discover our message is not being received, we need to turn the lens on ourselves and ask what we can do better. Maybe we put a sticker on the shirt of every kid leaving class reminding families that school is closed the next day.

If stakeholders keep asking a question again and again, then it's likely that the one meeting you held on an issue did not quite make a lasting impact. If the response to your communication is crickets, it's likely also evidence that something was lacking in your communications. Pay attention to that kind of feedback as a means toward sharpening your communication strategy. If we are listening, we can learn from each other, adapting as we go and getting better at realizing our common vision.

As we prepared to reopen schools in fall of 2020, I really messed up a town hall that was intended to inspire confidence from staff in communicating our path forward. I expected the town hall to serve as a sort of trial run for the all-staff communications that were planned for the following week during onboarding. Instead, the majority of the staff showed up and overwhelmed us with questions that we were unprepared to answer. It was a full-fledged waterfall moment. And I flubbed my framing, focusing on the positive impact our reopening would have on students and families who were counting on us, rather than acknowledging the fears of the group I was addressing. They needed to hear me say "We need you. And also, we've got you." It was a missed chance to strengthen community in a large-group setting (which I'll discuss more in Step 4). Fortunately, they trusted me enough to gracefully make it clear that I had missed the mark. I didn't respond as well as I wish I had in the moment, but I got a lucky chance at a do-over during onboarding, and I leveraged the feedback to dramatically enhance my approach.

The transferable takeaway is to be intentionally attuned to whether your communications are working. Build multiple channels to allow feedback to happen all the time. Don't delay. When people are not clear on what they have signed up for, they are unable to align their actions in service of the vision. Progress stalls.

We don't ask staff to wait for a formal performance review to know how they are doing, nor do we ask families and kids to wait for family conferences to discuss their progress. The best feedback is live feedback while experience is still fresh and its congruence with the vision still vivid. Then we can act on it with urgency.

Communication is a leadership burden. Our ability to achieve the outcomes desired is first dependent on our ability to communicate them, and why they matter, in a way that resonates with the audience. Is your communication strategy eliciting increased buy-in?

If we are successful in our communication strategies, families and staff will be in no doubt about what they have signed up for. They will be on the bus, to quote Jim Collins. The next step is to reinforce their membership by going beyond words to appeal to them viscerally, as I will discuss in the next chapter.

REFLECT ON YOUR PRACTICE

Be transparent.
- How do you proactively consider your audience and their needs, expectations, and questions?
- How do you acknowledge what you do not know or candidly share news of impending change, while still inspiring confidence in your vision?

Be clear.
- How do you compel the audience with the benefits of fulfilling the vision?
- How do you ensure the audience understands what they will be asked to contribute to fulfill the vision?

Be consistent.
- What core elements of your vision do you draw upon repeatedly to anchor your communications?

- How are key vision elements messaged in a way that people can latch onto (e.g., words, phrases, expressions, norms, catch-phrases, analogies, etc.)?

Be effective.

- How do you practice and test your messaging?

- How do you garner real-time feedback about how and if a message is being received?

STEP 3:

Signal Shared Identity

Working in the Bronx, you see a lot of Yankees hats. And shirts. And keychains. And windbreakers. And backpacks. When I travel, that familiar interlocking NY logo against a navy blue or pinstripe is everywhere I go. Even if they know next to nothing about baseball, most everybody knows what the logo represents. Put on a Yankees cap, and you signal participation in a shared identity of tradition and achievement.

The marketing department at the New York Yankees knows better than anyone that reinforcing a vision through shared identity is a job. It is not just about selling keychains. It is about being intentional in the ways people are invited into a tradition with physical objects and rituals.

For a generation now, the Yankees groundskeepers who come out to sweep the infield at the bottom of the fifth inning lead the crowd in dancing to the song "Y.M.C.A." And the fans on hand participate as well: grandparents dance with grandchildren; strangers dance with strangers. Maintaining the tradition deliberately aligns practice with the cultivation of shared identity. It is a signal that everyone understands with all five of their senses.

Physical objects, rituals, traditions, songs, and chants—all of them imprint on hearts and minds almost without the recipient noticing. The result is another elevation of will and commitment.

Once your stakeholders have signed on, reinforce their membership in whatever they signed on for by leveraging intentional cues or signals: visuals that remind them of their pride in membership, and rituals and traditions that provide them with an opportunity to express it.

In Step 2 I discuss how the purpose of strategic communications is to ensure that every message the organization sends out transparently, clearly, consistently, and effectively conveys or aligns with the vision you set for your organization. Too often forgotten is that there are also signals we send to reinforce the vision, often more powerful than words, because they are tangible and bring the organization to life— real life, physical life. Visible, intentional expressions of the community through naming, colors, the design of spaces, time-honored rituals and traditions—even the clothes on our backs—make the details of the vision manifest and offer people the opportunity to both feel and express that they are part of something.

HERE IS WHAT YOU ARE SIGNING UP FOR IN THIS CHAPTER:

* **Name people, name places, name concepts.** People, places, and concepts all require names that consciously express what your vision claims to value. There should be nothing accidental about the way things are named, whether it is classrooms or your mascot or anything else. Once you develop your naming

nomenclature, stick with it. Consistency is a powerful driver of commitment.

* **Bring people together with ritual and tradition.** Ritual and tradition knit a community together in a joyful, almost subliminal way that makes them feel part of something special and breeds a sense of ownership over the organizational identity. This feeling can endure across generations, but creating and sustaining it takes conscious collaborative effort.

* **Make your vision visible.** Visual cues reach deep inside us almost without our noticing. Everything about the way a school looks and how it feels to walk its halls should visually align the community with the vision for which they signed up. Physical artifacts such as print communications, anchor images, mascots, and swag should do the same. They should be applied methodically—the visual needs to mean something if you are going to display it.

Name people, name places, name concepts.

In the Bible, the first task that God gave Adam was to name things.[1] In our first school building, which you might call our own genesis, we had a gathering space we sometimes jokingly referred to as the café-tori-um-nasium. In our compact building it served all those functions. But its official name was the Nest. Because, of course, we are the Cardinals.

We are the Cardinals with intention. (And not just because being Cardinals allows us to create a deeply cool-looking mascot, which I will tell you more about in a moment.) We are Cardinals for two purposes: One, because we are educating our students to be models of the cardinal virtues. Two, because when we opened, we were given a generous lease on a vacant building by New York City's Cardinal Timothy Dolan. To be a Cardinal, then, is to embody virtue in general and the virtues of gratitude and generosity in particular. That is exactly what we tell anyone who asks.

---

[1] Genesis 2:19–20.

Naming our gathering place the Nest signals a sense of a single home for our family of Cardinals. We intend all the sensations associated with a nest—cozy, safe, welcoming, communal. We especially intend it for our kids, who seem to be far more attuned to signals than adults. Even before they learn to read, for instance, kids know what the McDonald's golden arches signal.[2]

In common with a lot of schools, and in common with charter schools particularly, Brilla names its classrooms according to a theme. Ours are named for universities. The intention was to get Brilla students accustomed to the idea that they might go to college one day. The naming was aligned with the vision.

It is not enough to simply name a classroom. We make the most of it. One of our founding teachers, Rachel Hayes, led a classroom named for her alma mater, the University of Nebraska. Nebraska's color is bright red, and fans of its teams chant "Go, Big Red!" and wear the team color everywhere. Those who claim association with the university proudly own the moniker "Husker," short for "cornhusker," a nickname Nebraskans have officially given themselves.

At Brilla, the members of the Nebraska classroom are Huskers. At our weekly pep rally, Huskers chant "Go, Big Red!" to announce themselves. They place a corn hat on the head of a scholar who best exemplifies elements of Brilla's vision. (They can also join an elective called "cow roping" by trying to lasso the legs of chairs turned upside down in their classroom. Where else would a kid from the Bronx get to have the experience of cattle roping?) At the end of the year, kids in the classroom write a letter to the next group of students who will be in that classroom with advice on "how to be a Husker."

In another school classrooms might be named after presidents, saints, or civil rights leaders, or simply Ms. Kopro's class or the chemistry lab. The point is that the name should signal something that can be made visceral. Throughout the year there should be days when

---

[2] "What Kids Know: McDonald's, Toyota, Disney," ABCNews.com, April 9, 2010.

each classroom demonstrates what it means to be named for a worthy person, place, or thing and how the name inspires them to live and work in alignment with the school's vision. We try to make all our names work just that hard.

Once you have developed your naming nomenclature, stick with it. Otherwise you will be missing an opportunity to sustain a connection to your school community that might otherwise endure for years just by invoking that name. That is the power of naming: Every time you speak the name, it invokes your vision. Every time kids in a class refer to the name in conversation, they reinforce their shared identity.

Bring people together with ritual and tradition.

Everywhere we go
People want to know
Who we are
So we tell them.
We are the Cardinals,
The mighty, mighty Cardinals
Ooo, rah, Ooh, rah

I love that chant. It is, shall we say, "borrowed" from the film *Remember the Titans*. You should hear us some time at our morning Bird Call. It is possible that we wake the neighbors.

Perhaps the biggest levers an organization can pull in signaling shared identity are the rituals that bring people together to make them feel part of something special. Sports teams are masters at this, employing chants, cheers, songs, hand motions, dances, colors, mascots, and more to create enduring traditions of membership in a family.[3]

---

[3] See, for example, Brian Scott Gordon et al., "Sport Fans and Their Behavior in Fan Communities," in Sports Management and Sports Humanities, edited by Kazuyuki Kanosue et al. (Springer, 2015). See also Bob Heere and Jeffrey D. James, "Sports Teams and Their Communities: Examining the Influence of External Group Identities on Team Identity," *Journal of Sport Management 21*, no. 3 (July 2007): 319–337.

There is a subtle but important difference between traditions and rituals. Traditions can include behaviors and artifacts passed among a community across generations sharing a common experience. Traditions give us a share of something enduring, something bigger than ourselves. Rituals, on the other hand, are specific actions reserved for specific occasions—graduation, say, or the first day of school.

It might seem that community rituals and traditions arise organically—that one day they are just there—but in most cases somebody needed to think them into existence.

Traditions and rituals are fun, but they need to be taken seriously. Leadership and staff should put real work and intention into the development of traditions and rituals that bring out in boldface the things we claim to value.

Declaring, for example, that you value community without designing school traditions that regularly bring the community together betrays a lack of intentionality. Or it reveals an impoverished idea of what communities do. Probably both. At Brilla, we bring our school communities together. And every time we gather it should employ particular music, particular physical materials, particular colors. The community should share the stories and purposes behind its rituals, deepening everyone's feeling of investment and of fellowship.

Repetition is crucial to the magic in tradition. For instance, think about big-time college football teams and their marching bands. They all have a traditional fight song. Returning alumni connect to the institution by singing the song alongside the eighteen-year-old first years. But the band also plays arrangements of newer songs. That way the tradition is both enduring and refreshed. This is intentional. It creates a feeling of a growing family that never gets old.

How great, then, is the opportunity for using those kinds of tools in a school full of children who have been wired by nature to need that feeling of family?

At Brilla we had a family whose oldest daughter was in our founding kindergarten class. She had two younger siblings who used to practice our songs as toddlers. They wanted to be ready when it was their turn to go to school and become a Brilla Cardinal. It was a special moment when they ceremonially received their Brilla T-shirt at their first home visit. (We have the video.)

Staff need to be full participants in the creation of rituals. Shared investment in the care and cultivation of the school's rituals yields a shared sense of belonging and shared ownership over the organizational identity. This is work that should not be top down.

It was staff, for example, who invented our annual Classroom Chant Competition, which is what the name says it is. It is intended to collaboratively create signals of shared identity with students, families, and staff. We create a compilation video of staff performing a chant when it was first created and later during homecoming week, when it is chanted by an entire class dressed in the college colors of their classroom. The pride is palpable.

We pay attention to rituals that signal shared identity among staff as well. For example, staff also created our RAK party. RAK stands for "random act of kindness." The party is intended to bring together specific teams from different grades or program elements. The teams collaboratively design a custom activity to celebrate and deepen their connections. Themes have spanned from luaus to murder mysteries, minute-to-win-it challenges, to life size reenactments of childhood games (imagine Candy Land, where you are the token moving through a creatively fashioned candy forest).

Twice a year all of our schools convene for a more structured community-building tradition. Our winter event is comparatively formal, with the option of bringing a guest—a spouse, significant other, family member, or the like. The spring event is more relaxed—an outing to a park, say, or a baseball game. Staff members are explicitly encouraged to bring their children. That reinforces our vision of a place where staff can bring their full selves to work.

Families are integral to school traditions and rituals. Without families there is no school community. The logic of this is so obvious it hardly needs stating. Families are included in the big moments that our school puts on, of course, like our Costume Carnival or Fall Festival. They actively participate in events like the Cardinal Cotillion, a K–2 formal dance for students to which they bring an adult role model as their companion. Then there is our 3-8 State Exam Party, where we celebrate the completion of exams under a banner theme chosen by the student council. Families serve as chaperones.

Our traditions involving families are not just the big get-togethers. There are smaller ongoing events, such as our regular Coffee and Conversations sessions for families. Chants like the one I gave you above? Many of them grow out of our weekly Family Challenge, an alternative take on weekend "homework" that gets everyone in a student's home involved. The intention behind Family Challenge is to provide families with an opportunity to work on something together, strengthening relationships in the home while also participating in the school community.

There is a sustained return on these investments of time. The student who writes the chant and their family are super excited that their chant is chosen. The student's class is excited. So is the grade. Every time the chant is performed, the school receives an adrenaline rush. The community, through all its spokes and subgroups, is brought together and rejuvenated.

Make your vision visible.

When the New York Yankees opened their new stadium in 2009, the architects were careful to make the place feel like the beloved old stadium built in 1923. Most famously that included the beloved façade that ringed round the rafters. Just seeing that façade was enough to link fans across the generations. It symbolized everything the community of Yankees fans held dear. The façade continues to be an anchor image for fans, wordlessly communicating what it means to be a Yankee. The ways we use physical space is another way of signaling identity.

Everything about the way a school looks and everything about the way it feels to walk its halls should remind the community of the vision for which they signed up. The design of physical space conveys how we feel about vision, whether we intend it or not. And the best part is that one swift effort can serve its signaling goal for a significant period of time with minimal maintenance required. Do not miss the opportunity.

Part of Brilla's vision is an educational experience inspired by the classical tradition. Therefore we work to make the design of our school spaces honor a traditional aesthetic that minimizes modern design features. Depending on your vision, you may go a different way. That is absolutely fine. The point is to make your spaces intentional expressions of your vision.

The effect of a building on the people who work in it all day should be, frankly, delightful. Consider the effect of a stairwell with fluorescent lights versus one with bright incandescent lights—which one lifts your spirit? One signals safety, while the other communicates something almost menacing. Which of those signals aligns with your vision?

Hallways

We have all been in buildings that give off a bad vibe. They do not grip us, they do not make us want to be there, and they do not lift our hearts.

Hallways are usually our first impression of a place, so here is our rule: make hallways beautiful. Not beautiful in the conventional sense of pretty. Beautiful in the classical sense of beauty as an arrangement of parts into a harmonious whole. Be opposed to clutter, we say to our staff; do not persuade yourself that an aesthetic cacophony is a joyful noise.

Cleanliness communicates order, among the highest of the classical virtues. An ordered space encourages an ordered mind. Just as we make a schedule to audit the good order and cleanliness of our physical space, we also make a schedule for auditing hallways for their eloquence in expressing the school's identity.

Classrooms

Why put anything at all on classroom walls? It is heresy to even ask most teachers such a question. A teacher who would leave their classroom walls naked is a rare exception. Since you are making that choice, whatever you put up should have a reason behind it, an intention aligned with your identity, anchored in your vision.

Consider the common practice of posting a classroom's values. Are they in harmony with the values of the whole community? (It is surprising how frequently they are not.) Assuming they are aligned, the declaration of values should be in a place so prominent that teachers and students cannot help referring to them every day.

A core element of Brilla's vision is honoring the dignity of individuals, so it is nonnegotiable that in the classroom there is a dedicated space where individual students are held up as exemplars of specific classroom values. In our schools this is typically a bulletin board with the four cardinal virtues spelled out. Right beside each virtue is a photograph of a child in the classroom who has exemplified it. Other kids will be added through the year on the recommendation of their peers. The practice is meant to be dynamic and participatory. It reinforces a feeling in students that this is their classroom. That is their name is on the wall. That is their picture. Their place in the vision is visible. They have a share in the identity of this place.

Teachers should have autonomy in designing their bulletin boards; school leaders should not micromanage this. But aesthetic alignment to the school vision should be nonnegotiable.

To get a sense of how deliberate we are about this, in their annual reviews our teachers have an evaluation metric for classroom appearance. They may not be artists by nature. But if they are intentional, they can get better at that part of their job. They can go to colleagues for help, or draw from our supply budget to realize what they imagine.

Classroom décor should prioritize alignment with both the curriculum and the broader vision for the school community. Everything that goes up on the wall or gets set out on the windowsill, even the colors we employ, should signal our shared identity by referencing the vision we have all signed up for.

The staff lounge

Think of any book or film set inside an elementary school, and it is amazing how prominently the teachers' lounge features in the plot. Lounges are a haven for staff and a place of mystery for students. For a space with so much mystique—and so much potential for encouraging a shared identity—calling it just the lounge does not do the place justice.

We want to use our staff lounge to declare an intention about the place where teachers gather as true colleagues. That is why we call it the Cardinal Lounge. (There is the power of naming again.) Every Brilla school has a Cardinal Lounge. Staff knows it is a space for renewing and for forming relationships, not for working. If we want staff to know each other, then we need to design a place that encourages colleagues to eat lunch together, not alone in their classroom. It goes back to the influencer model: provide a structured place and time for staff to meet, and you make it harder to isolate behind a desk.

The décor of a Cardinal Lounge is inspired by the Central Perk coffeehouse set from the TV show *Friends*—I kid you not. That implies a couch, for one thing. We want a coziness that feels like a second home. This creates specific expectations about furnishing. That includes making it a student-free zone. If we want adults to form relationships that are not exclusively centered on work, then they need to be free to talk about their wider adult lives.

At our first school, the furnishings of the Cardinal Lounge included a copy machine…until we realized that this did not back up our vision of a collaborative staff building relationships that transcended work. How could it, with the copier banging away in the background when people were trying to have a conversation (or that incessant beeping when it jams)? More than that, the copy machine was a temptation to work. It impeded our intention to support a shared identity.

By making the Cardinal Lounge a comfortable, welcoming place, we send a signal to staff that they are valued and that their sense of connection to one another is valued, both core to our particular vision.

Print communications

Visuals that reinforce our vision and shared identity are not limited to physical space. They can also come in print form. In our school calendar, for example, or in the newsletter kids take home in their backpacks, you will find our shining B logo, the use of red, the treatment of headings, the consistent font—all of it is done with intention.

A flyer about a dance, for example, needs its construction to reinforce its purpose. Usually that means employing colors and images that excite the senses of children so that they will want to attend. You do not excite kids with long paragraphs in Times New Roman. It is the same reason the average couple spends hundreds on wedding invitations. The words need to be accurate, but it is the visual design that bears the responsibility for signaling the vision for the wedding itself.

Choices about print structure send further signals. For Brilla, this means that materials must be pleasing to look at and hold in the hand, free from weird jump cuts, poorly cropped photographs, and typos. If we fail at these seemingly small things, we send an unintended signal that we do not uphold our vision of pride in our work. We are not reinforcing expectations of quality.

Anchor images

An anchor image is a nonverbal cue to the values we share in common. If we want to represent courage, we might depict a common association, such as a lion. Or we might put up a photograph or quotation of someone from history who defended an unpopular cause. Wisdom might be represented by an owl. Self-control could be a hand over the heart. Our norm of "Principle over Preference" might be illustrated with a rendering of french fries versus vegetables.

The concept of an anchor image is a cousin to the way we apply consistent phrases, analogies, and so on in our communications. Both make our vision more accessible and easier to remember, increasing the odds that it will be implemented.

Whatever anchor images you choose need to be audience-appropriate signals of your ideas and easily understood. They should be explicit and applied consistently.

Mascots

We do not have any official school teams (yet). But from day one we have had a mascot: a large red Cardinal. If your school does not have a mascot, is there a reason why? Especially in a community whose foundation is children, it would be a missed opportunity not to have one. Kids love mascots, and it gives the school community a physical manifestation to rally around. If you do have a mascot, you should be able to say out loud how your choice aligns with and furthers your school's identity.

At the start of every school year our Cardinal arrives to school in a limo. The Cardinal escorts the scholar who was previously crowned Cardinal of the Year for best exemplifying our core virtues. At the end of every school year our Cardinal makes an appearance at our Shine Awards event, celebrating academic and virtue growth and achievement. The Cardinal also comes to celebrate its birthday. The intention behind that ritual is to mark the number of years since Brilla opened.

In between we employ our mascot sparingly. The kids do not see the Cardinal at every school occasion. When the mascot appears, it signals to everybody that the moment is a big deal.

When we designed our school logo, we wanted people to see it shining. We are Brilla, after all. We paid similar attention to mascot design to be sure it aligned with our vision for the community—high-flying, joyful, noble, steadfast, nurturing. When we create awards and recognition rituals, we brand them with the mascot's image. We respect the power of our big red bird to signal shared identity and convey the values of our community. We would never put its image on anything arbitrarily.

Swag

A while ago we had a staff member who wanted a budget for coffee mugs with the Cardinal's image on it. We were not automatically opposed to the idea. What we were opposed to was that this staff member was overcommitted to handing out mugs, T-shirts, pens, and other Brilla-branded items as tools of identity building. People could have furnished entire homes with all that stuff. Abundance was diluting the impact of our swag.

Creation and distribution of school-branded stuff should have an aspect of ritual about it. To begin with, it should be well made. If we want our school to be associated with quality and intentionality, then even the most basic piece of swag should embody—literally embody—those two qualities. Better to give out fewer pens and have them be well made. In other words, no junk that breaks before you have even had time to lose it. Holding a piece of school-branded swag in your hand should deliver a feeling of pleasure. It should be functional. The color palette should delight you and remind you of your membership.

To hold value, as economists say, swag should not only be made well but also intentionally limited in supply. The scarcer a thing is, the more we have to earn it, the more we value it. If a shirt or a coffee mug is meant to signal membership in something special and yet we hand them out to anybody who comes along, how does that signal shared identity?

At the end of their first full year of service to Brilla, staff are presented with a well-made Boathouse jacket. Every jacket is tagged with the name of their Brilla school across the back. Their last name is monogrammed on the front. With each additional year of service a star is sewn on the jacket sleeve, somewhat the way a high schooler earns a varsity jacket and then adds patches to it over time. Those of us who have been around a long time beam with pride as we walk the hallways in our star-studded jackets.

Weather permitting, staff members wear those jackets all year long, especially to school rituals and celebrations. The jacket and its annual embellishment are a visible representation of service to the community.

And they look great. Staff members are so proud of those good-looking jackets that they have been known to ask if they can order one to give as a gift. The answer is always no. The jacket needs to be earned. Putting it on your back needs to cost something more than money; otherwise, it is just a piece of clothing. (Families take an interest in the jackets too. They can earn one by participating in the Family Involvement Committee.)

Staff wardrobes also have in common a T-shirt with our last names on the back and two digits representing the current school year. The front design is reimagined every year but is always intentionally modeled after a sports uniform. This piece of swag is meant to provide a signal of shared experience as a team during a particular school year. For example, I might notice a colleague wearing a T-shirt with a "17" on the back (representing 2017) and be reminded of the year that we grew from one school to three.

Some swag is only for families. Families can earn a Brilla Voices shirt, for example, by speaking to external audiences, such as during meet-and-greets with prospective Brilla parents or information meetings with funders and board members. To be seen wearing that shirt is to signal one's identity as part of a group of parents dedicated to sharing the Brilla story. We want to inspire others to earn that good-looking shirt.

All of us need something—something solid like a school memento or something we feel in our hearts like a ritual—to remind us of our shared identity and to signal that to others. That is especially true for children and the adults who educate them, because that sense of belonging is prerequisite to active participation in the school community and its goals.

At Brilla, we signal our shared identity on purpose. And we do it with intentionality. We have put deep thought into how we can further our vision through our nomenclature and rituals and traditions. We have worked to make our vision tangible in the physical aspects of our school. And we have worked to make the signals meaningful by paying attention to, for example, their placement, consistency, and scarcity. This deliberate use of signals has helped us create a foundational condition of engagement with our school's vision that will last for years, a concept I describe in the next section.

REFLECT ON YOUR PRACTICE

Name people, name places, name concepts.
- How is nomenclature decided and assigned to align with your school's identity and to reinforce the vision?
- How do stakeholders engage with and apply the nomenclature?

Bring people together with ritual and tradition.
- How are rituals and traditions designed and developed to align with your school's identity and to reinforce the vision?
- How do stakeholders engage with each tradition?

Make your vision visible.
- How does your school's visual aesthetic align with your school's identity and reinforce the vision?
- How do your school's swag, print media, and other branded items align with your school's identity and reinforce the vision?

PART 2

ENGAGEMENT

STEP 4

Create the Conditions of Connection

Research has shown that soldiers do not fight for big ideas or grand feelings of patriotism. Instead, they fight for one another. They would do anything rather than let down a friend.

While still a staff instructor at the US Army Command and General Staff College, Robert Reilly wrote that "Soldiers' sense of obligation to comrades and their desire to obtain and retain respect allows them to endure what otherwise would be unbearable… Without the cohesion of the small group, leadership, no matter how charismatic, will not allow soldiers to withstand the pressures of combat."[1]

It is common to hear educators refer to the grind of the school year as a battlefield. During the COVID-19 pandemic we got a taste of how

---

[1] Robert J. Reilly, "Confronting the Tiger: Small Unit Cohesion in Battle," *Military Review*, November–December 2000.

close that analogy could be. Teaching primary school students at this time felt at times like a life-and-death commitment. Brilla's staff, our families, and most of all our kids will forever share the experience of working through the pandemic together, of wanting to be in the same building together despite the hardships, of wanting to see the vision fulfilled.

The pandemic spotlighted the essential role of committed humans in a classroom as never before. Anyone who experienced all-virtual attempts at education during those years can describe the many ways that virtual education left all concerned feeling impoverished, neglecting our human need for presence.

In the summer of 2021 McKinsey & Company released a study suggesting the pandemic left K–12 students on average five months behind in mathematics and four months behind in reading by the end of the 2020–2021 academic year. The crisis widened preexisting opportunity and achievement gaps, especially among historically disadvantaged students. There was demonstrated impact not just on academics but also on the broader health and well-being of students, and their mental health specifically.[2]

Even without a McKinsey study we knew we had to get students back in the classroom. For most of the 2020–2021 school year, the majority of New York City students at schools both public and private remained virtual. But the Brilla vision, which holds that there is no substitute for in-person care and attention, would not permit us to distance ourselves from our kids. Pandemic or not, we had clients—our scholars—whose life prospects would be meaningfully determined by the education they received. We had families who needed us. They made it clear that they wanted in-person learning.

Physical distance eliminated the human connection that makes education live. Without human interaction—with a teacher, with one

---

[2] Emma Dorn et al., "COVID-19 and Education: The Lingering Effects of Unfinished Learning," McKinsey & Company, July 27, 2021.

another—kids were not getting the literal visceral experiences that stay with us all our lives.[3] They did not have the joy of turning to a classmate and saying, "I can't believe she just did that. That was so cool."

Brilla reopened in late September 2020 with 60 percent of families opting for in-person instruction. And it stayed open. Staff and teachers kept coming to work despite the virus. Two things kept them going: commitment to the vision and their connection to one another.

That kind of connection is built with intention.

Connection cannot be left to chance. Committed relationships, personal or professional, do not just happen. They need to be facilitated.

HERE IS WHAT YOU ARE SIGNING UP FOR IN THIS CHAPTER:

* **Build community in large-group settings.** A unique energy is derived from bringing people together in large groups. Sharing a well-crafted moment as a full community reminds people that they are not alone in the work. It reinforces a shared sense of mission and the mutual accountability that is derived from each participant having a critical role to play.

* **Leverage large-group collaboration as a tool for connection.** When done correctly, large-group collaboration allows the broad school community to engage in ways that elevate the quality of their work in support of kids, first of all, and in support of their own professional satisfaction.

* **Build intimacy in small-group settings.** Relationships are born from intimate interactions. Putting people in the same place at the same time, under structured conditions to facilitate interaction, creates an opportunity for them to unearth common interests. Participants move beyond typical workplace concerns toward genuine human connections anchored in the values

---

[3] Emma Dorn, Bryan Hancock, Jimmy Sarakatsannis, and Ellen Viruleg, *"COVID-19 and Education: The Lingering Effects of Unfinished Learning,"* McKinsey & Company, July 27, 2021

of the vision. Reinforcing these relationships both within and across stakeholder groups provides for increased synergy across the organization as a whole.

* **Leverage small-group collaboration as a tool for connection.** Deliberately designed opportunities for collaboration in small groups can fight the tendency toward isolation within our individual domains. Stakeholders are able to tap into alternate sources of inspiration and learning by accessing the gifts of others to fulfill the vision.

Build community in large-group settings.

Year four of Brilla's existence was the year we learned the outcomes of our first state achievement tests. The results were not good. Families, of whom we had asked so much, looked at us like we had broken a promise. And still we had to ask for their continued trust. Staff was demoralized. I still feel the personal anguish of that moment.

And yet, we had to act. We modified our curriculum and asked kids and staff to commit to a longer school day. We changed the terms of being on the bus. The very proposition of our school model hung in the balance.

August onboarding is our traditional time for asking everyone to recommit to signing up for our bus. The year after those disappointing exam results, there were also new staff from the two new campuses we were about to open. On the last day of onboarding, I checked my email a final time before making my closing presentation. The state exam results had hit my inbox.

I will never forget how scared I was to open that email. But not to look would have violated our norm of principle over preference.

The results were outstanding. In a single year Brilla had improved student achievement outcomes by 10 percent, which is unheard of.[4]

---

[4] Even before COVID-19, change in the reading scores of American students on statewide tests was essentially nil year over year. Lauren Camera, "America's Kids Earn Disappointing Grades on Nation's Report Card," *US News & World Report*, October 14, 2021.

Quickly I updated my closing PowerPoint to showcase the results along with photographs of students who failed the year before and were now testing at or above grade level.

The response was electric. Staff stood on their chairs and chanted "On the bus! On the bus!" The significance was not lost on new staff who had only just started their jobs at Brilla. At the end of the presentation, all of us went off together in celebration.

That was a Hollywood moment. Imagine if I had chosen to simply send an email sharing the results. The opportunity to bring the whole community physically together to share our success, and the memories and bonds that still endure from it, would have been lost.

That day was not simply a reward for working longer hours or enduring the mental drain of learning new curriculum. It was a testament to the efforts of the entire community of staff and families. The amplified connection born from sharing that moment together elevated everyone's sense of commitment.

In tough times—perhaps especially in tough times—performance is strongly determined by our bond with one another.

Prerequisite is a shared understanding of the vision. But on its own that is not a sufficient condition. To sustain commitment there must be trust in leadership and in colleagues. There must be bonds of shared experiences, affection, and the feeling that if we lift each other up, we will make it to our goal.

Feelings of connections are often happy accidents of proximity. Good leaders do not trust in happy accidents to elicit feelings of connection. That would be like believing in magic.

The concern of most organizations is making sure employees understand their jobs and have all they need to do them. These are areas leaders believe they control. Work friendships, in contrast, are assumed to be intangibles, nice to have but coincidental to the mission.

On the contrary. From connection we derive a sense of duty to one another. The vision becomes personal. Success becomes a shared desire across the organization.

I will give you what might seem like a silly example of what I mean, except that the consequences for the organization are not silly at all.

At the beginning of each year we conduct what we call a co-teacher wedding. It is the moment when we celebrate the matching of two teachers who will co-lead a class for the year. We make it a big deal. The paired teachers walk down the aisle side by side, the principal officiates, and the school social worker signs the "marriage certificate." The pair are presented with a wedding gift: a flag for the college associated with their classroom. No one just watches. Everyone has a role to play. All become invested in the success of each pairing. (Two people in particular who "married" as co-teachers subsequently fell in love and married for real. When I heard that, I remember feeling like I should retire right then and there.)

Leverage large-group collaboration as a tool for connection.

Those mega moments that inspire connection in large groups need not be limited to communications exercises or fun events. Collaborative opportunities prove equally powerful for creating the conditions of connection. Collaboration ought to be commonplace in schools. Too commonly it is not, and in fact it is a leading cause of turnover.[5] Collaborations in large groups give us a look at the gifts colleagues bring to work, colleagues whom organizational structures might ordinarily keep us from meeting.

In many schools and organizations, professional development events are notorious for being snoozefests, with a talking head at the front of the room droning on about something for which the application is hard to see. If you want to succeed at building or redirecting your culture, do not fall into this trap.

Our schools do not have professional development events. Instead, we have Mission in Progress meetings—the MIPs I described in Step

[5] Desiree Carver-Thomas and Linda Darling-Hammond, "Teacher Turnover: What It Matters and What We Can Do about It," Learning Policy Institute, August 2017.

1. The chief characteristic of MIPs (apart from their purposeful name; again, be intentional about naming in a way that promotes the vision) is that they provide staff with the opportunity to come together around key elements of our vision.

Get people involved in these collaborative events in a way that is meaningful, engaging, and not cheesy. At one MIP we might do a deep dive on one of the four cardinal virtues and how we experience these as adult professionals. Or we might conduct a Socratic seminar so that everyone has a shared experience of what a seminar looks like when it is done well. We may use an MIP as a communications opportunity, such as our annual State of the Schools presentation modeled after the State of the Union address. The intended outcome is that staff walk away with a deeper sense of connection to the vision, of course, and an improved skill to fulfill it. But our other intention is that the experience of being in the room, with so many others who share your passion for the vision, creates a fervor that deepens it.

Among students, building connection with the larger group goes on at school every day. Core lessons are often taught to the whole class all at once. Teachers have mounds of evidence to reinforce the value of having students learn together.[6] We want our families to share that same sense of connection, so we create opportunities to make it happen. A good example is an initiative of ours called Parent University.

We know families are hungry for knowledge about how to support their children's education. At Parent University we might spotlight the Love and Logic model, for example, to explain how we apply it in the classroom and how it might be reinforced by families. In advance of state exams, we explain Brilla's approach to test prep while sharing resources for families to use at home. Our monthly Coffee and Conversations events bring families together in a large group to learn about topics that may be of value to their families — how to promote health

---

[6] William Damon, "Peer education: The untapped potential," *Journal of Applied Developmental Psychology*, October–December 1984, Pages 331-343

and wellness in the home, speaking with kids about the potential dangers of social media, etc.

Just as with the examples for staff and students, families emerge better equipped to execute on the vision and reinforced by the knowledge that they are sharing the joys and hardships of parenthood with many others, even if they do not know them all by name. These family events have borne out the inherent power of large group collaboration—more than 60 percent of families routinely attend these voluntary Parent University events after work and on weekends.

Build intimacy in small-group settings.

We do not need research studies to tell us that personal connections are an enduring source of happiness in a life or in a job. (Although there certainly is an abundance of such studies.[7]) Losing touch with the specialness in one another is among the serious challenges of managing growth in any organization but especially in schools. When the organization is small, the conditions for creating relational intimacy are inherent. As an organization grows, opportunities to deeply connect become scarcer.

Since the 1970s Gallup has administered what it calls its Q^{12} survey. To date the Q^{12} has been administered to nearly three million people around the world. Gallup's tool uses a dozen statements to take the measure of employee engagement, especially the engagement of an organization's most talented people.

The most provocative question in the Q^{12} is "I have a best friend at work." Gallup readily admits this question generates skepticism from clients.[8] It is a question anchored in an idea of intimacy, which might at

---

[7] See, for example, Andrew E. Clark et al., *The Origins of Happiness: The Science of Well-Being over the Life Course* (Princeton University Press, 2018). For a general account of the Harvard Grant Study of how human beings derive meaning from life, see Scott Stossel, "What Makes Us Happy, Revisited," The Atlantic, May 2013.

[8] Bill Murphy Jr., "Gallup Calls This 8-Word Question Its 'Most Controversial' Ever. (But a New Survey of 2,000 Workers Shows It's What Employees Care about Most)," Inc., October 17, 2019.

first feel extraneous to the business of an organization. That would be wrong. Education is such a personal business for all concerned.

Getting bigger need not work against the maintenance of small-group communities that are such fertile vectors of connection. Even within a large organization, small groups benefit from opportunities deliberately created to inspire personal connections.

Not all of our tools for creating connection across the organization are explicitly connected to the immediate work at hand. We created, for example, a group to bring together staff who shared the experience of being a working parent. The group was composed of teachers from different grades and staff from different roles inside Brilla—teaching, operations, administration, anyone. The purpose of this small group was not simply to get to know one another. The purpose was allowing individuals to share an authentic experience of the people with whom they work.

At first the members did simple things like share recipes and talk about local family-friendly activities. But quickly the group became a way of seeing a side of one's colleagues that would not otherwise be visible. Soon the members were talking about the challenges of managing their simultaneous commitments to Brilla alongside their vulnerabilities as parents. What had at first seemed unrelated to the professional sphere became another structure of support for the vision.

The success of this pilot spurred a new initiative called Focus Groups. Under that broad title, we invited staff to lead programming for a small group of colleagues across working teams, on nearly any type of topic that may be of shared interest. Some ideas that emerged were collaborative in nature and directly tied to work outcomes. Examples might be a new-teacher support group, basic Spanish language skills, book club, or pedagogical best practice shares. Others were more akin to the parents' group, tapping staff personal interests that—at first—appear to have no direct connection to our work as educators: hip-hop yoga, crochet, personal finances.

We provided the time, space, and resources for these groups to flourish. The outcome across all the diverse offerings of focus groups was that staff members developed intimate connections with each other. These were connections that would reinforce their commitment to Brilla, allowing them to share in their celebration of the high moments and carrying them through the challenging ones.

Before COVID-19 we worried about how Brilla's rapid growth would affect our ability to create conditions for intimate connections to be formed, not only across work domains but also across different geographic campuses. Overnight, Zoom became a commonplace tool in all our lives. It made cross-campus bonding easier than it would have been in person. Being remote ironically afforded new opportunities to grow close.

One way we overcame the limitations of being remote was through what we called Brilla Bunches. These were groups of roughly ten people across campuses and across roles. In each bunch, members took turns being facilitators and leading the conversation. We insisted on a plan for these conversations. Again, be intentional! Do not fall into the trap of thinking that setting up small group meetings will inherently breed intimacy and connection. I address this more in Step 7, "Ensure Impact," but it is not enough to simply set up small groups and force them to speak with one another at set times. The likely outcome of that will be a waste of everyone's time and possibly resentment at being forced to do it. You have to be intentional and take the next step of structuring these group conversations.

After a burst of virtual gatherings during staff onboarding, Brilla Bunches would reconvene approximately once a month for just thirty minutes—time enough for intimate moments to occur. The evidence of impact? One day the staff of our Brilla Veritas campus arrived to find the building had flooded during a heavy rain. The news was shared with our other campuses. A logical reaction from a member of the nonimpacted campus would have been "Gee, that's too bad." But through Brilla Bunches, a teacher at a different campus had become acquainted with an operations team member at Veritas, and instead of simply reacting and moving on with her day, she texted the Veritas member to check in and to see if there was anything she could do to help. Because of Brilla Bunches, two people who otherwise may never have had occasion to know each other formed a connection; trouble at a different campus had a human face.

There are notable stories of staff who have asked colleagues to be godparents to their children, bridesmaids at their weddings, and travel buddies overseas. They did not teach in the same grade or even teach the same subject. They had no connection at all before their friendships blossomed as a consequence of a deliberate effort at creating connection.

As with any of these culture-building concepts, our efforts are not limited to staff. Brilla pursues the creation of a web of connection in all our stakeholder groups, but especially among students. To use a simple example, if we kept our kids in assigned seats all day long, then students on opposite sides of the room might never know they shared a mutual love of dinosaurs. That's a simple example that we scale to the organization at large.

On Fridays, for instance, Brilla offers elective clubs to students across grade levels. Teachers, usually in pairs, decide what electives to offer based on their personal passions. This has the bonus of bringing staff together in collaboration. Past examples have included cheerleading, Lego building, student council, and cow roping. Student relationships flourish in these intimate moments, and they acquire a mentor among teachers outside their classroom.

Our annual block party—the Mott Haven Celebration—is an opportunity for families to connect in small groups within a large-group setting—a twofer. This block party is a good example of the dynamic interplay between creating bonds between stakeholders within both large and small groups. The celebration is one of the largest events Brilla hosts. It is not just for students and their families but for the wider neighborhood around our schools, with which we might not otherwise meaningfully interact. It literally brings the community together in a joyous setting to celebrate the Brilla vision.

Central to the celebration is the Mott Haven Cultural Showcase, which is designed to show off the cultural riches of our neighborhood. We host activity booths and bring in local community organizations and businesses to spotlight their products and services. A local radio station hosts the event.

But as large an event as this is, it presents an opportunity to create opportunities for bonding within smaller stakeholder groups. For example, we ask families to sign up to work in shifts to help host. The signups intentionally appeal to families' varying interests and comfort levels. Some may want a more passive role, like supervising the sidewalk chalk station. Others may desire to actively plan for and host one of the country booths. Parents who volunteered to lead the booth representing the Dominican Republic set the standard. They wore traditional dress, brought artifacts, and planned craft activities. Those parents had students in different classes and grade levels, yet the act of working together on the booth created the condition for them to form a bond born of shared heritage. When the call for volunteers was launched the following year, they revealed that they had already been collaborating on ideas to take the booth to the next level. And for a bonus connection, the staff member who volunteered to serve as a partner in the activity booth also grew close with these parents. The intentional structures created the conditions for connection not only within but also across stakeholder groups.

And they had fun. But the conditions for creating small group intimacy can be born from a professional context as well.

Leverage small-group collaboration as a tool for connection.

In many schools, small-group collaboration is the most inevitable opportunity for connections to be born. One example would be the collaboration that occurs among teachers who work on the same grade level team. These teachers often prep lessons together, analyze student work, and share resources because they share the experience of teaching students from the same grade. The members of a grade level team would probably collaborate anyway without much of a push from school leadership. Leadership's role is to erase the boundaries that inevitably pop up even within a single grade.

At Brilla, for instance, teachers on a grade level team engage in a practice called lesson studies. This small-group experience allows the transfer of effective teaching practices, which are too often considered just a gift, something some teachers are born with and others are not. How does my peer create a hook that engages a student's attention? How do they guide students through common misconceptions that might take them off course? The experience of collaborating with one another in small groups can provide answers to these questions, creating collective efficacy and stronger team bonds.

Teachers also come together to collaborate by reviewing student achievement data or brainstorming around how to best support individual students' learning needs. Meaningful collaboration engendered so much trust that teachers advocated to have some of their students receive reading instruction from their colleagues instead of themselves. They wanted to leverage the expertise of the colleagues on their team to meet the individual learning needs of students from across the grade level, putting their own students' achievement in another's hands.

At the middle school, grade level teams might be organized by content. What that means is that math teachers from multiple grade levels might, for example, analyze how a concept taught in fifth grade is foundational to a more advanced skill learned in sixth grade, ensuring that there is a through line in how the concept is taught.

The members of small teams acquire knowledge of one another's skills and of one another's character. The act of working together intimately allows people to experience each other's gifts. As Reilly observed, engaging in challenging and relevant tasks bonds small groups together "in a sense of mutual accomplishment and the shared conviction that all members have overcome a tough test. Only by developing the trust and confidence in each member will the small unit develop cohesion."[9] The vulnerability required for a staff member to say "This is what I'm struggling with; can you help me?" or "This is a strength of mine, and I'd like to share it with you" furthers the basis for trust. They learn to trust one another in particular and not just in general.

This trust ramifies across the organization so that in one of life's hard moments—for instance, when we tell staff we need them to come to school during a pandemic—they trust that someone is focusing on their well-being. The trust forged among small groups coalesces into a larger web of connection. It's the "degrees of separation" effect—even if I don't have a close relationship with a particular person in the organization, I am close with someone else who does, and that increases my level of investment. From a sense of duty to one another we are fully present. We root for one another to be successful. The vision becomes personal.

Are Brilla people sometimes skeptical of the steps we take to create the conditions of connection? Yes, they are. Sometimes even people on the bus are skeptical—until they see the effect of connection on performance and professional satisfaction.

In creating the conditions of connection, it is not enough to dream up opportunities for groups, both large and small, to come together. The intention behind these must be active, and the vision must be embedded in all of it, even if only indirectly. Simply hoping that lightning will strike is not a strategy.

Connection among members of the school community is what makes them show up and bring their best selves to school. Students benefit. Families benefit. Staff benefits. Because they are on board with the school's vision and feel connected to its members, the conditions are now in place to invite their active participation.

---

[9] Reilly, "Confronting the Tiger."

REFLECT ON YOUR PRACTICE

Build community in large-group settings.
- What opportunities exist for whole groups of stakeholders to share meaningful experiences?
- How do your whole school or large group gatherings build community in ways that transcend the day-to-day work?

Leverage large-group collaboration as a tool for connection.
- What opportunities exist for a whole group of stakeholders to work together toward a vision-aligned goal?
- How do your collaborative opportunities for a whole group of stakeholders deepen professional connections and further the vision?

Build intimacy in small-group settings.
- What opportunities exist for small groups (within and across domains or stakeholder groups) to share meaningful experiences?
- How do your small group gatherings facilitate connections that transcend the day-to-day work?

Leverage small-group collaboration as a tool for connection.
- What opportunities exist for small groups (within and across domains or stakeholder groups) to work together towards a vision-aligned goal?
- How do your collaborative opportunities for a small group of stakeholders deepen professional connections and further the vision?

STEP 5

Create the Conditions of Participation

In 2014 Cisco Systems was a former dot-com superstar laboring to get its mojo back. In the never-ending war for talent among technology businesses, Cisco was struggling to create a culture that attracted—and, more to the point, retained—great talent.

About that time two operations managers in Cisco's London office observed what they considered a broken connection between the Cisco employee experience and the company's goals for itself. To their credit, senior managers took those observations seriously. Looking across the organization, they saw that the same disengagement characterizing the London office also afflicted the company's operations around the world. It seemed built into its structures.

Cisco responded by formally surveying employees about key moments of their experience, from their first impressions on the day they started work to their compensation levels to the user experience of office technologies. What they learned was that the feeling of connection was broken between leadership and the people with the power to make the company thrive. People were, if not cynical, detached.

The result was what Cisco now calls its People Deal, a formal delineation of mutual responsibility between the company and its employees that, in the view of one analyst who follows the company, has created an "intentional" culture of connection and innovation.[1]

As Cisco CEO Chuck Robbins has said, "Our future as a company is going to be defined by how we drive our culture." The structures of the culture had to be rigorous and purposeful. Good people had to be inspired to stay.[2]

The People Deal worked. In the years between 2019 and 2021 Cisco was ranked either number one or number two on *Fortune* magazine's list of "Best Places to Work." Oh, and the company's share price rose from about $22 at the start of 2014 to $58 in August 2021.

As Cisco learned, there can be no bystanders in a vision-driven organization.

There is a reason why the titles of Steps 4 and 5 ("Create the Conditions of Connection" and "Create the Conditions of Participation") are parallel. The intention is to emphasize that neither connection nor participation can be left to chance. It is a leader's responsibility to create the conditions to enable both.

It does no good to create the conditions of connection if individuals in the school community enjoy relationships with one another but are permitted to be passive spectators in the fulfillment of the school vision, passengers asleep on the bus.

---

[1] Patrick Moorhead, "Cisco's 'People Deal' Exemplifies Its Cutting Edge Commitment to Employees," *Forbes*, August 8, 2018.
[2] Michelle Fox, "The 'Great Resignation' Is Altering the Workforce Dynamic—Maybe for Good," CNBC, November 3, 2021.

HERE IS WHAT YOU ARE SIGNING UP FOR IN THIS CHAPTER:

* **Distribute leadership.** Distributed leadership is an idea that sometimes gets pushback from people who argue, "If everyone is responsible, then no one is responsible." On the contrary, a distributed leadership model ensures that high-level vision is balanced with ground-level context, and it applies practice to the belief that culture is driven by team members who feel that their specific role is integral to fulfillment of the vision.

* **Create mutual accountability.** A shared sense of ownership and accountability to outcomes is a core driver of synergy and performance. Interdependent goals ensure that resources, ideas, and energies are actively shared rather than withheld. But they do not arise organically.

* **Activate free choice.** Giving individuals scope for free choice makes it hard for anyone to say they are, let alone to feel like they are, passive participants in their own lives or in the life of the organization. If it's not happening *to* you, the tendency toward despair, anger, or apathy is replaced by a sense of agency and empowerment.

* **Design structures of influence.** When designed with intention, structures of influence produce a virtuous circle of individual action harnessed to the collective vision of the whole.

* **Activate strengths.** The objective of feedback should be to inspire performance, not to score it. Performance increases dramatically when people feel they are applying their strengths in service of a worthy cause.

* **Make everyone feel like a keeper of the culture.** The ideal state for any organization is a condition in which everyone feels accountable for ensuring the proliferation of the culture. Amassing an entire community as keepers of the culture is far more impactful to outcomes than entrusting it to a limited few who cannot rightfully be in all places, at all times.

Distribute leadership.

When Brilla was still in start-up mode, our vision was so strong we could taste it. But we also knew that the vision would be dead on arrival if we did not imagine structures for making the "why" of culture visible in ways that engaged all the members. If we wanted Brilla to live and grow, we had to expand our ideas for engaging the vision beyond the room in which the founders sat dreaming their new world.

From the beginning we had the intention of capturing the best in all of us in service of the vision. It started in a basic way, naturally, with blog posts soliciting ideas from staff members. That was the right impulse. But it was not enough.

Any organization in start-up mode is fizzy with ideas. As organizations mature it becomes more challenging to keep the fizziness going. There is a risk of things becoming routine, of sticking with what seems to have worked in the past. The sense of personal engagement weakens. We begin to feel like bystanders.

When I sat in the principal's seat I was aware of the temptation to behave as if I knew better than anyone. I was a founder, after all, and from where I sat I had the widest perspective—didn't I?

Had I given in to the temptation to be the boss, to insist on being the smartest person in the room on every issue, all sorts of wisdom in our organization would have gone untapped. With the best intentions in the world I would have made decisions (and OK, sometimes did) without the context that people charged with implementing those decision can provide.

Unwillingness to distribute leadership is not always just a matter of ego. When we are new to the job of managing, it can be hard to find the confidence to acknowledge that other people may know more than you. This insecurity might make you feel that asking for guidance reveals weakness. You might give yourself the excuse of saying there is no time to get a second opinion, that it would be quicker to just do what seems to have worked in the past or what feels most logical— logical to you, that is.

Managers may be reluctant to delegate to others, especially those new to managing. But you should not blindly define delegation as asking people to do more work. Effective delegation is about encouraging people to grow and to feel integral to the success of the mission. Effective delegation shows the organization that everyone counts and that everyone is expected to participate.

There will be times, of course, when leadership needs to act without recourse to partnership and participation. During the COVID-19 crisis there were initiatives that demanded quick choices. In some cases, distributed leadership went out the door. We suffered because of that. We ended up not having good insight. People were unhappy because the choices we made were not responsive to what was happening on the ground. We should have known. It was written into our essential practices. We had all signed up for it.

At such times leaders are drawing on the trust they have built. To use Stephen Covey's term, they are drawing from a kind of emotional bank account shared by members of the organization.[3] Draw on the account too often, and you risk bankruptcy.

To minimize the risk of this happening too often, we conceived and implemented a formalized distributed leadership structure called a Guiding Team. The purpose is to hold Brilla leadership accountable for ensuring that the right range of voices are invited to the table of participation, particularly when considering a new initiative. A Guiding Team is a representative group of staff from various roles and different campuses. It is formed to garner proactive input regarding the impact of a new initiative rather than reactive feedback. Early indications from the Guiding Teams, focused on, for example, crafting procedures for reduced social distancing guidelines, redesigning instructional minutes, or envisioning a distinct model for upper middle school students, have signaled they are a transformative condition of partici-

---

[3] Stephen R. Covey, *The 7 Habits of Highly Effective People*, 30th anniversary ed. (Simon & Schuster, 2020).

pation. There were few hiccups when these enumerated initiatives hit the ground.

Vulnerability and humility as a leader are preconditions to authentically distributing leadership. Done right, a distributed leadership model ensures that high-level vision is balanced with ground-level context. It brings to bear representation from the same people who feel the impact of an initiative, helping to ensure that every person sees how their participation matters a great deal to fulfilling the vision. Lip service to this concept won't cut it. But seriously implementing and making real a distributed leadership model across an organization will help achieve a potent result: mutual accountability.

Create mutual accountability.

Political scientists sometimes speak of what they call the free-rider problem. You might also call it the bystander effect. Free riding is a calculation some members of a group may make that they can shrug off personal responsibility because others will pick up the slack.[4] All of us have had the experience of how poisonous such disengaged members of a group can be.

One individual's disengagement undermines the commitment of the whole. Pretty soon we start to question whether we are missing something, whether we are right to be enlisting our hearts and minds with such conviction, if that no longer seems to be the norm. This is precisely the reason for working to structure the conditions of participation.

Even in organizations with weak culture, members will default to some form of collective activity. Good organizations actively pursue collective activity in pursuit of interdependent goals.

Say I am a member of a grade team. If I am required to write lesson plans for a subject (math, for instance) that will be relied upon by all the other teachers in the same grade level, it will inspire in me a

---

[4] See, for example, James Andreoni, "Why Free Ride? Strategies and Learning in Public Goods Experiments." Journal of Public Economics 37, no. 3 (December 1988): 291–304.

sense of responsibility to my peers and to a whole grade's achievement. Leaders should structure this type of interdependence as an essential element of their school design. Doing so will inspire interlocking responsibilities among stakeholders.

The commitment to interdependent goals permits no free riders. Everyone is expected to take initiative.

In pursuit of 100 percent attendance at family conferences, we enlist families and teachers. Everyone knows that, mathematically, each class has to achieve full participation for the goal of 100 percent to be achieved. There is no averaging to 100 percent. This is mutual accountability.

Families respect the goal enough that they help one another when, for example, a family runs into a snag at home and needs childcare to be able to attend their conference. I recall a time when a parent, after attending the conference for their own child, traveled to another Brilla family's home to care for their sick toddler so the mother could attend the conference of her older Brilla student. Out of a shared sense of pride in the mission, they lifted each other up.

Teachers promote the goal of 100 percent attendance internally—there is literally an email chain that goes around to all staff, with each co-teacher pair replying once they have reached that objective. It builds momentum as we advance closer and closer to our target, while simultaneously reinforcing the expectation that every class must achieve it.

Activate free choice.

When an individual has a sense of choosing to participate—a personal sense of ownership, of leadership, of responsibility—it affirms their sense of worth. It affirms their dignity. And it makes it harder for anyone to feel as if organization decisions are happening *to* them. They cannot be passive participants in their own lives or in the life of the organization.

We work hard at developing the sense of free choice in our kids. A primary way we do it is by modeling it as the adults around them.

Families who get accepted in Brilla's lottery decide to accept a placement or decide not to. We are not their district public school; they have other options. In every open house we explain to families what kind of organization we are. We are up front about acknowledging that our partnership model might not be for everyone. They may choose a school that is a better fit for their family's needs. They may leave at any time.

Before anyone—student, family, teacher, anyone—gets on our bus, we preview our responsibilities to one another. All of these stake-holders, myself included, sign a document called the "Commitment to Excellence." This is an idea borrowed from another charter network, KIPP Schools. It lays out what we sign up for: the essential mutual commitment made by the school, families, and teachers to uphold the vision.

If ever we find ourselves in a spot where we do not agree completely on the shared expectations we have set, the "Commitment to Excellence" provides a common reference point. If a party to the compact still objects, that requires a deeper discussion. We seek to understand whether the disagreement represents an opportunity to advance our bus forward, by inviting participation to clarify, improve, or adjust the expectations, or whether the misalignment is more fundamental, in which case perhaps Brilla isn't the right place for them. In other words, our bus may no longer be their bus.

Once during my time serving as a Brilla school principal, I had a family that actively resisted the expectation of their attendance at family conferences. If I recall correctly, they were also annoyed with us for upholding dress code standards for their child. They were feeling adversarial. They were feeling acted upon.

"Even if you come to our house," they told me, "I'm not answering the door."

I referenced the "Commitment to Excellence." I recalled the specific section under "Family Commitment" that communicates the expectation of attendance at conferences. I anchored the "why" in our vision, reminding them that they had agreed to be a partner. I activated their free choice; I reminded them that this is a two-way street, that their signature affirmed that this was the vision they had signed up for, even if their level of commitment had changed. I was serious about what our organization stands for. I wanted them to be serious too. In the end we recommitted to what was required of all of us. The family's choice to enlist in Brilla's vision brought us back to the center of our relationship.

When rising fifth graders make the move to middle school, there is an associated ritual in which they refresh their expectations. At this ceremony we adapt the version of the "Commitment to Excellence" that they "signed" as incoming kindergarteners at their home visit. Then students, too, activate their free choice to recommit with a fresh signature.

The transcendent idea of the "Commitment to Excellence" is that we all choose to be part of a broader team and vision, which begets accountability to one another. For staff, this is built into the structure of their performance reviews. Principals at Brilla are evaluated by how well they uphold our "one school" philosophy of building their school while also supporting the network as a whole. A principal can achieve amazing results within their own silo, but if they are not engaging with other schools to share their practices, they will have a low score on this portion of their evaluation. If that feels like the wrong aspiration to a principal, then we have transparent and supportive conversations about whether Brilla is the correct fit.

These are not insincere conversations. We recognize the gifts and skills of the staff member and have a mutual interest in seeing them leveraged for the benefit of children. We strive to get to a place where they can embrace all the core elements of Brilla's vision. Even if we are unsuccessful, we support, accept, and encourage their choice to apply their gifts and skills in service of students elsewhere.

This "one school" philosophy extends to teachers as well. For example, co-teaching pairs are evaluated as a team with regard to the family relationships indicator, informed by surveys directly from families. Even if one is outstanding at making positive phone calls, distributing resources, or sharing class updates, the weakness of the other impacts overall engagement. So they receive the same score. The message it sends is "I'm accountable for our class."

Concern for honoring individual agency shapes the way we facilitate performance reviews as well. It enables us to have targeted conversations about whether performance is a skill issue or a will issue (to use the language of the influencer model). Conversations about subpar performance are never focused on punishment. That would make a mockery of the idea of choice. We focus on opportunities to elevate a staff member's impact. What can you spotlight that is going well? Can you build on it to inspire growth in an area of weakness?

We have had staff, for instance, who separated from Brilla because they disagreed with our Love and Logic approach to discipline. Implementing Love and Logic is challenging, and we say so in detail when new staff members join. Some prefer a more traditional system of rewards and consequences. They may spend months fighting Love and Logic in their classrooms before accepting that we meant it when we named it as core to our model of high performance.

There will always be difficult moments in the pursuit of any vision. When they arise, it helps the organization enormously if there is a generalized feeling of personal agency. Negative watercooler conversations are subdued by a general feeling that what happens in the organization is a manifestation of choices we all make. "It starts with you," as we like to say. We are all invited to participate.

By and large, when staff members exit our organization, they do so in a positive way. For instance, they communicate the timing and reasons for their departure with transparency and adequate lead time, they refer other candidates, or they come back to visit during our Mott Haven Celebration, graduations, or other community events. We try to make separations a two-sided choice, the same as we would with families. There is no need for any of the parties to be angry. The vision gains nothing from anger. For another thing, an angry departure honors no one's dignity. Finally, we might miss an opportunity to learn something. And we never forget that the whole time the organization—kids, other staff, families—is watching.

We talk about departures in terms of mutual understanding. We want the choice to separate to make sense to all parties. In the times when it doesn't, we strive to honor the staff member's dignity and reiterate that our decision is informed by Brilla's mission and vision. This is a micro example of our earlier discussion under "Say What You Know." We empathize, and we convey our understanding of the consequences of this decision on the particular individual. But we anchor the decision in our mutual understanding of what we all signed up for.

We have all made a choice to participate in realizing the vision. This is the message healthy organizations should send and send again: we choose to be on the bus. The result of that choice is a corresponding responsibility to make the bus the best it can possibly be. Stakeholders, then, require a clear path to direct their renewed motivation and energies to help elevate the vision. We call this structured influence.

Design structures of influence.

People choose our bus because they hope to make a difference in the lives of children. If they feel unable to make that difference, they would be remiss not to go somewhere else where they might have more power and more influence.

One of the qualities that Jim Collins observed in the successful companies profiled in *Good to Great* is their openness to new ideas that come from within their organizations. If people in your organization have an idea, how do they get an audience for it? Is there a clear path that everyone understands? Or are there hoops to jump through? When team members contribute ideas that are implemented, are they celebrated broadly in ways that illustrate the pathways to influence for other members of the organization?

An organization's structures of participation should tap into the gifts people bring in service of its vision. In our school, for instance, we have something called program leads. Typically, these are talented staff and teachers who raise their hand because they have a new idea they would like to try. In a way, program leads are a spiritual cousin to Lockheed Martin's famous Skunk Works.[5] Skunk Works is the pseudonym for Lockheed's Advanced Development Program, which commissioned a research and development team to quickly develop a jet fighter for the US during World War II. Launched in 1939, Skunk Works is such a storied tradition at Lockheed that one can even buy swag featuring its distinctive cartoon skunk (proving once again the staying power of mascots). Although a registered trademark, the term has since become a casual nickname for any innovation initiative undertaken outside of an organization's conventional structures.

You can describe such mechanisms for inviting participation in organization building as structured influence. They are paths that allow anyone with a specific skill to apply it to a need the organization has—or to a need the organization does not yet recognize it has.

Like the members of Skunk Works, programming leads are usually teachers with a big idea they would like to build out. They make a detailed pitch to leadership. If they get a green light, they get a stipend, they get development time, and they recruit a cohort of like-minded colleagues to partner on the idea. (There is that relationship piece again—people grow closer by working on a passion project together.) Meanwhile, teaching remains their core job.

Not long ago a Brilla staff member piloted a new block of learning designed to give students a structured opportunity to explore their personal backgrounds, whatever they might be. Her pitch to her leadership team was that it would encourage students to celebrate the qualities that made them distinct.

---

[5] See, for example, Ben Rich, Skunk Works: *A Personal Memoir of My Years of Lockheed* Back Bay Books, 1996).

One unit, for example, was on "hair love." It was intended to get kids comfortable in acknowledging and celebrating the beauty of different textures of natural hair—an important lesson for students as they enter the self-conscious years of adolescence in a society where they are exposed to straight hair as the norm of beauty. Its wider lesson was in service of Brilla's mission to recognize and celebrate the dignity in every individual. It was aligned with our vision.

The initiative was met with such praise on its Brilla campus that we committed to rolling it out across all our schools. All because one person had seized the opportunity offered by a structured path for influence.

People in organizations notice things like that. They signal that an individual need not be a friend of the boss to get their ideas heard. The influence of this signal on the desire to take initiative is enormous. It gives credibility to the vision's claim that everyone has a growth path.

A school organization's structures of influence should not be limited to staff. They should provide pathways to families and students too. For example, we provide a clear path for families to bring their concerns to members of Brilla's Family Involvement Committee, a representative group of family members empowered and entrusted with representing the parent perspective to school leaders during monthly meetings. This path is utilized. At our flagship campus, families who arrived early in the morning were attuned to how dark it was outside of our buildings; the lack of lighting posed a safety risk. They brought this issue to school leaders through the Family Involvement Committee. This clear path for influence yielded the intended result. Brilla dedicated money to the installation of new floodlights outside of our buildings, improving safety for all stakeholders. This seemingly small act had a profound impact: it signaled to families that their participation was as valued as we always say it is. It affirmed that their advocacy was taken seriously and that they are integral to fulfilling Brilla's vision.

Building structures for influence matters to an organization's career development pipeline and to the retention of both staff and families. A clearly defined process for making an impact demonstrates that the organization takes innovation seriously. It acts on what it claims to value.

The reward is more innovation and more ideas to advance the vision. It is a virtuous circle of individual action harnessed to the collective vision of the whole.

Activate strengths.

People who believe they are using their strengths every day are three times more likely to report having an excellent quality of life and six times more likely to be engaged at work.[6] Research by Gallup, which boasts of studying thousands of work teams and leaders, managers, and employees over the last half century, has published empirical evidence that the more hours a day that adults—and, in our experience, children—believe they are using their strengths, the more likely they are to report the following:

- ample energy
- feeling well-rested
- being happy
- smiling or laughing a lot
- learning something interesting
- being treated with respect

Inspiring participation is the logic behind what is commonly called strength-based coaching. In the broadest terms, strength-based coaching elevates areas where people are doing the right things and spotlights these for the organization. The concept is in harmony with the influencer model. It inspires others to emulation and to take initiative on their own.

---

[6] Brandon Rigoni and Jim Asplund, "Developing Employees' Strengths Boosts Sales, Profits, and Engagement." *Harvard Business Review*, September 1, 2016. See also Brooke Fernandez and Sarah Houle, "An Effective Strengths Program: Cardinal Health Case Study," *Workplace* (Gallup), May 18, 2015.

When an organization delivers feedback to its members—a performance review, say, or a report card—it should produce more than just a numerical score. (Numbers can be useful indicators as long as we do not fall into the trap of a false precision.) The centerpiece of any feedback mechanism needs to be the story it tells about the person on the receiving end.

The objective of feedback should be to inspire performance, not to score it.

At Brilla, for example, families get a narrative of how their child is doing, not just a grade. Staff get perspective on their progress—who they are as professionals and how they contribute to our school community. Creating these narratives formally—twice throughout the year—is an investment of time. It is worth the investment it takes to produce.

If the only thing feedback communicates is "get better," not only is that not dignified, but it does not inspire better performance. If all a review does is beat people on the head, they will do the minimum required to get the other person to stop beating them on the head. This is as true for children as it is for adults. To make it worse, unrealized talent may be lost for no sensible reason.

You may be thinking, "most performance evaluations I have experienced go significantly beyond this and are structured to ensure a balance of strengths with growth areas." And you may be right, at least with regard to what's on paper. And yet, I have sat in on a fair share of performance review conversations where the discussion moved straight to the growth areas with only the most limited acknowledgment of strengths, despite what was in the written evaluation. Intentionality in activating strengths must be built into all elements of the evaluation process.

Smart feedback practice tells us stories about ourselves we may not even know. Even in discussions of growth areas we *intend* feedback to be a positive experience. We *intend* feedback to be opportunities to amplify our strengths. We *intend* it to be a recognition of every individual's dignity and potential for agency. We *intend* all this for a pragmatic reason: because it works.

One of our teachers was a star at just about everything except for family relationships, which are a core element of Brilla's vision. On a number of observable indicators pertaining to family relationships, they scored a 2, or "approaching standard," on a scale of 4. When they applied to be a team lead, we explained that a minimum score of 3, "meeting standard," was required on the family relationships indicator in order to be eligible, as modeling this for other members of the grade team was a crucial element of the team lead role. For a great talent like this teacher, being stymied in their ambition to grow could have been demoralizing. Instead, we framed it as an opportunity to activate their strengths in new ways.

Between one evaluation and the next—just four months—this person raised their family engagement score to a 4. They became a team lead that year and have since been promoted to other positions of leadership. It was one of the most inspiring efforts toward growth that I have witnessed, and it is a testament to their standard-setting commitment to constant learning and to the thoughtful, inspiring framing and partnership of their coach, another Brilla star.

By using feedback to inspire participation, organizations spend less time on the defensive, less time in a deficit mindset, and less time navigating HR challenges, performance improvement plans, and the like. To bring it home, the ultimate condition of participation is one that enables all members of the school community to share responsibility for proliferating the culture, rather than relegating the responsibility (and sometimes burden) to a select few.

Make everyone feel like a keeper of the culture.

Healthy structures of participation are characterized by their interconnection. One supports another, all support the whole.

A good example is what our school has dubbed Culture Club. This is a sort of organizational senate to plan, facilitate, and champion the culture initiatives of the school. Over the course of a school year every member of our staff sits on Culture Club. (That's a lot of people, and yet it is that critical, so we scope it out before the year even begins.) This ensures there is always representation from each team at any given time, and that all members of the staff community are presented with a condition for participation.

When a staff member serves their term on Culture Club, they feel like they are representing their peers. They take it seriously. They are not just improving existing ideas; they are also responsible for renewing them. Culture Club makes everyone feel like the "why" of culture is everyone's preoccupation.

One iteration of Culture Club, for instance, did outstanding work in reshaping our celebration of themed months like Hispanic Heritage, Black History, and Women's History. We intended these to be deeper than mere gestures and more genuinely collaborative in their celebration of the people who make up our school community. Brilla families were brought to the stage during our weekly pep rallies to share the prized aspects of their backgrounds. It was a collaboration informed by our vision of a place where all are both welcome and uplifted.

In a way, Culture Club represents a roll-up of all the concepts discussed in this chapter for engendering participation. To get its work done, Culture Club brings people together from across domains, distributing leadership for initiatives and enabling members to activate their strengths. The group, rather than an individual, is collectively responsible for the outcomes of their initiatives, begetting mutual accountability. By accepting their seat at the table, group members utilize a clear structure for influencing the next level of Brilla's culture initiatives. As the initiatives are underway, their participation and endorsement are both essential in promoting buy-in from the peers they are intended to represent. And there is a bonus: by participating in a small group format with colleagues from across the campus, the conditions of connection are put in place.

If an organization wants everyone to have a part to play in realizing the vision, it needs to create paths for allowing that to happen. These paths are the conditions of participation.

If an organization wants people to feel individually essential to the organization's success, then each member requires clarity about the roles they can and must play in that success. Individually they need to know those roles matter a great deal to realizing the vision. There needs to be mutual accountability to one another.

And if an organization builds these structures, it needs to make clear by its behaviors that the invitation to participate is genuine—that all gifts are accepted, the subject I take up in the next chapter.

REFLECT ON YOUR PRACTICE

Distribute leadership.
- How are representatives across layers of your organization empowered to shape high-level decisions?
- How is ownership of any given initiative shared across layers of the organization?
- How do leaders in your organization garner ground-level context?

Create mutual accountability.
- How is each person/team responsible for fulfilling your organization's high-level goals?
- How is each person/team responsible for one another's achievement?

Activate free choice.
- How are individual contributors reminded of their ability to impact change?

- How are individual contributors prompted to respond to perceived barriers?

Design structures of influence.

- What are the pathways in your organization for people to have their ideas heard and considered?

Activate strengths.

- How are strengths prioritized and leveraged when supporting and motivating high performance across stakeholders?

Make everyone feel like a keeper of the culture.

- How is each person/team responsible for uplifting and proliferating your organization's culture?

- How does peer accountability promote your organization's culture?

STEP 6

Accept All the Gifts

In public corporations, no one would ever go on the record as opposed to inclusivity. Doing so would be a really bad look. But let's be honest. Do investors really care?

Turns out the answer is yeah, they do. And for hard-nosed reasons. A steadily growing body of evidence correlates inclusivity with higher profitability and rising share prices.[1]

In 2019 Stanford University published a study showing a describable link between companies reporting improvements in the diversity of their organizations and the performance of their stock price. When the diversity news was positive, the share price went up.[2]

---

[1] See Rebecca Greenfield, "When Companies Improve Their Diversity, Stock Prices Jump," *Bloomberg Business*, September 17, 2019. See also Emily Glazer and Theo Francis, "CEO Pay Increasingly Tied to Diversity Goals," *Wall Street Journal*, June 2, 3021.
[2] Katia Savchuk, "Do Investors Really Care about Gender Diversity?" *Insights by Stanford Business*, September 17, 2019.

Combine that with an environment in which the war for talent affects every kind of organization. Organizations with a culture of inclusivity and a describable purpose beyond profit are most likely to attract and hold on to talent.[3]

Whether your business is education or developing software, success is dependent on the creativity and smarts residing in your organization. To miss the multitude of gifts that a collection of people brings to work would be to miss so much that is crucial to innovation and to flourishing.

And still, for all their good intentions, organizations struggle to get inclusivity right.

I am aware that anything touching on these subjects can feel like a third rail on a dozen different levels. A big part of the reason is that the motivations of organizations pursuing inclusivity are not large enough. Unwittingly, inclusivity is often conceived as a defensive tactic—a tool for avoiding problems—when it should be understood as a source of enormous value to an organization.[4]

One of the virtues Brilla teaches is gratitude, thankfulness for the gifts life provides. That guides us in the ways we think about inclusivity, which strives to honor the dignity of all members of the community by creating a warm and welcoming culture to which everyone is authentically invited to share their individual gifts in support of the vision.

Leadership may devise conditions of connection and conditions of participation. They may feel there are open seats at the table, but other members of the community may be reluctant to sit down. If people do not feel welcome, if they do not feel seen, they may be hesitant to use even well-intentioned structures of connection and participation. They may be afraid that the things that make them different—the way they look, the way they speak, the way they think—might cause them to be

[3] Jim Harter and Vipula Gandhi, "7 Things We Learned about US and Canadian Employees in 2020," *Workplace*, June 15, 2021.

[4] Frank Dobbin and Alexandra Kalen, "Why Diversity Programs Fail," *Harvard Business Review*, July–August 2016.

perceived as in some sense "off the bus." The responsibility of leadership, then, is to express sincerity in both word and action that they accept all the gifts.

....

HERE IS WHAT YOU ARE SIGNING UP FOR IN THIS CHAPTER:

* **Extend a sincere welcome.** Every action must convey that everyone is invited. If inclusivity does not mean everyone, then it does not mean anything.
* **Invite the whole person.** Align intention with the lived experiences of the people around you, so you can engage their gifts without causing harm to their dignity. To do that you need to know them as full human beings—without being intrusive.
* **Make it safe to share gifts.** For the structures an organization builds in support of connection and participation to be genuine, they need to be *safe,* specifically in a psychological sense.
* **Welcome feedback as a gift.** Great leaders see the person standing in front of them. They recognize when a gift is being handed them. If the organization isn't open to those gifts, then why bother offering them?
* **Seek input as a gift.** Welcoming input from everyone harnesses the collective genius of an organization. It wins the support of the people the organization depends upon to make the vision live. It is efficient, because it allows gifts to shape the path before the momentum of roll out becomes prohibitive.
* **Embrace challenge as a gift.** It is in the hard times that a culture is strengthened. It helps in navigating the hard times if we keep front and center the gifts that individuals can offer, even if only indirectly.

Extend a sincere welcome.

Working in a city-based network of schools, you have to be prepared for just about anything. For example, at the beginning of one school day we arrived to find narcotics users outside our buildings. Of course, we were concerned first and foremost for the safety of our kids.

But in order to achieve this, we responded to the person using narcotics by honoring their dignity. We explained respectfully that there are children present—would they please relocate? We offered to help find assistance if they needed it. The remarkable thing is that most people are so hungry to be treated with dignity that they respond with less drama than you might imagine.

Treating people with dignity sometimes unearths unexpected gifts. We noticed a resident on our block, for example, who was making the cleanliness of the street in front of our school his personal mission. He could often be found sweeping up food trash spilled from an opened bag or clearing the sidewalk of debris. That was the gift he was offering. It would have been very easy to put our heads down and ignore this gift or redirect him by insisting that our custodial staff be left to do this job. Instead, we got to know him, and it turned out his nephew was a Brilla student. His mission was therefore personal. We accepted his gift and hired him as a handyman. In the years that followed, he tackled projects from painting to planting, and he was first on the scene to help when a power outage nearly prevented us from entering the school building minutes before students were due to arrive. He even thwarted some mischievous squirrels who were trying to feast on chicken eggs we were hatching in a kindergarten classroom.

At such moments, consciously or not, we send signals about our willingness to put our vision to the test. The lesson we are modeling for anyone watching these exchanges—kids especially—is that the rule still applies: everyone is welcome. If inclusivity does not mean everyone, then it does not mean anything.

Our definition of an inclusive welcome incorporates some of the same things a typical HR department might mean, including equitable recruiting, bias training, and tools to minimize cultural misunder-standings. But two aspects of our approach to inclusivity are critically different.

One, inclusivity is not restricted to conversations in the HR department. It is evident everywhere.

Two, inclusivity includes hospitality—not in the usual sense of serving coffee to visitors (though it includes that too) but in a commitment to offering sincere welcome to everyone, those who are on our bus and those who are not.

People in all organizations notice action and measure it against words. A principal who collects trash off the floor or tidies the hallway displays signals that these small gestures of welcome are not beneath anyone. We watch for that same quality of welcome when we recruit new staff. Candidates will of course be friendly in their interview; they are motivated to make a strong impression. But how do they respond to the people around them who are seemingly uninvolved in the interview process? Are they kind toward the custodial staff, teachers they encounter in the lounge, the staff who run our main office?

In the ways we pursue a culture of hospitality at Brilla, we have gotten some of our best ideas from studying best practices at the Ritz-Carlton hotels[5] (which, as it happens, were also influential in the intentional culture of welcome at Apple Stores[6]). These include a warm, sincere greeting; anticipation and fulfillment of each guest's needs; and a fond farewell. From day one, we thought about how people would be treated when they came to Brilla, a credit to fellow founder Yeime Valle. If a family walks in off the street with a question about middle school, we are not going to send them away saying, "Sorry, we're an elementary school." We would say, "We're new here, but let's see what we can learn together about middle schools in the neighborhood."

---

[5] Joseph Mitchell, *The New Gold Standard: 5 Leadership Principles for Creating a Legendary Customer Experience Courtesy of the Ritz-Carlton Hotel Company* (McGraw-Hill Education, 2008).

[6] Carmine Gallo, "How the Ritz-Carlton Inspired the Apple Store," *Forbes*, April 10, 2012. See also Kate Taylor, "Chick-fil-A Consulted Ritz-Carlton and Fine-Dining Pro Danny Meyer on How to Make Its Customer Service Better Than Any Other Fast-Food Chain," *Insider*, September 5, 2019.

If they came to the main office, they saw photos of our kids and their families all over the walls.

People who greet visitors—and that can be any of us—show respect in the way they speak to others. They address visitors by their names if they know them. Visitors concerned for their child should not be made to feel awkward because they cannot engage in English. This operating philosophy is why our main office staff is mostly multilingual.

The intention behind this concern for hospitality is to show the families in our community that we value them. If one is suffering from food insecurity or a disaster like a house fire, we want them to feel comfortable coming to us for support. If they are starting a new business venture, like one of our moms selling her custom-decorated gourmet cookies, we want to be their first customer. Without rooting hospitality in respect for dignity, these would be mere techniques. They would be manipulative.

Observing that leadership is serious about welcome inspires a willingness to take advantage of the conditions of connection and participation. Showing care for people creates a sense of mutual investment in the vision. The consequence of anchoring mutual purpose in a commitment to welcoming is higher performance.

Invite the whole person.

I love surprises. When I plan a staff event I try to include something that will lend a bit of the unexpected, of novelty. The aim is stimulating engagement.

Once, for example, I led everyone into Midtown Manhattan for a surprise community-building event in Times Square. I did not reveal the location until our travels were underway, wanting to build their anticipation about where we might be headed. We finished right on time at five o'clock, but for some the enjoyment of the activity had been undermined by anxiety over being so unexpectedly far from school. What I had not considered was that there were staff who had to get back to the Bronx by five thirty to pick up their kids from daycare.

Now they were going to be late. This would have a negative impact on them and on their child.

We were a young staff at the time, and many of us did not have major responsibilities besides work. This personal perspective obscured my view of the people I worked with. That was an important evolution in my practice. That trip to Manhattan was one of several such moments that taught me to apply a relational perspective to all my interactions in school. I was learning to align intention with the lived experiences of the people around me. To do that I needed to know them as full human beings.

Today, if there is a school event that will require us to change geographic locations, not only do we share this well in advance, but we also build in commuting time to get back to our home base. In some cases, we provide carpooling budget. If participation requires more of our team than a typical workday, we get it on the calendar months in advance.

We still have the expectation that all of us will participate in community-building events; this never changes. But experience has inspired us to include a devil's advocate in our planning to challenge our logistics, particularly in respect to elements that further inclusivity such as attention to dietary needs or physical accommodations. We pay attention to the consequences of plans for the people affected by them, not the other way around. This requires us to gain deep knowledge of who those people are.

Individual members of your organization should aspire to a genuine appreciation of one another's individual backgrounds. They should have an active interest in the answer to the question "Who are you?" That is different from probing anyone's private life. (That would be an exceptionally bad idea.) Appreciating another's background in the sense I mean is a richer definition of inclusivity than I think most organizations know how to pursue.

One practical—and noninvasive—tool for understanding the substance of one another is the Life Map. This is not an idea that originated at Brilla, but one we have learned to esteem as a best-practice tool.

At the beginning of the school year every member of staff gets five minutes to map who they are for the rest of the group. It is up to them what they want people to know. We might include basic biographical information. We share things you would expect, such as hobbies, favorite sports teams, musicians, pastimes. Most of us go deeper than that in describing ourselves. Members commonly describe their cultural backgrounds, family situations, or formative experiences growing up. They talk about the traditions and motivations that shaped who they are. They conclude with an anchor image, a single visual that best captures who they are as a person.

A different kind of example are commitment meetings. Think of these as the inverse of an exit interview. Both events include questions about the experiences people have at work, how the interviewee feels received by the organization, and their perspective on their manager's view of them. Brilla's questions are aligned to what we care about in the vision. Both, in their way, are about feeling known. The power in the commitment meetings, held at the beginning of each school year, is that they enable us to learn about and apply insights to improve the staff experience while they are still on our bus.

Seeing one another in that kind of depth changes how leaders make decisions. It changes how we understand one another's contributions. It changes how we assess whether the actions of the organization are aligned with our goal of being open to and encouraging staff contributions.

Leaders can encourage members of their organization to feel fully welcome by inviting them to share the gifts they offer. They can invite people to show as much of themselves as they feel comfortable doing— *without* crossing boundaries. They can make it feel safe to show up.

Make it safe to share gifts.

Leadership can devise conditions of connection and conditions of participation. It can convey sincere welcome in its practices and invite people to show up by placing open seats at the table. And still some members of the community may be reluctant to sit down. This is frustrating for everyone.

The structures an organization builds in support of connection and participation need to be authentically inviting. That means they need to be *safe,* specifically in a psychological sense.

Willingness to reveal ourselves to other people and to see them fully in return is more than just a virtuous goal. Paul Zak, a leader in the field of neuroeconomic studies, has shown that the brain chemical oxytocin is catalytic in stimulating feelings of safety and connection within a group. The release of oxytocin in the brain can be stimulated in teams with what Zak calls "pro-social leadership behaviors," such as empathy and compassion.[7] When organizations trigger these emotions, the brain's engagement with the work of the team goes up. So does trust in one another. Trust gets the job done.

And yet, instead of trust, I am often conscious of an undercurrent of fear in the relationships inside many organizations: fear of making a mistake, fear of getting yelled at, fear of being embarrassed for saying the wrong thing, fear of being the wrong thing.

Creating psychological safety is a challenging endeavor, as most of it is driven by our responses to people's gifts, in moments both large and small. And we are human; we are fallible. So we have incorporated a few strategic systems to help alleviate the pressure on a specific individual to uplift inclusive practices all day, every day.

In our elementary school classrooms we have co-teachers. And in our middle school, students rotate to classrooms led by different

---

[7] Paul J. Zak, *Trust Factor: The Science of Creating High-Performance Companies* (AMACOM, 2017). See also Paul J. Zak, "The Neuroscience of Trust: Management Behaviors That Foster Employee Engagement," Harvard Business Review, January–February 2017.

teachers. Students also build relationships with social workers, operations team members, and their fine arts and applied arts teachers. These are not just the casual kind of relationships; they are the deeper ones fostered from leveraging the conditions of connection. These structures provide benefits for content specialization and differentiated instruction for students, but they also ensure that every child has the opportunity to learn from and be affirmed for their gifts by a number of influential adults.

Our perceptions of what constitutes a gift are shaped by who we are and by our experiences. A quality that one might find endearing, another might find annoying. Where one perceives limit testing, another sees self-advocacy. The point is that diversifying the number of people to whom we offer our gifts increases the likelihood that someone will see the gift for what it is: a gift. That breeds safety.

Staff similarly benefit from supportive structures to ensure that they can feel safe to share their gifts. Our staff is managed and developed by multiple leaders. For example, a teacher might be developed in math pedagogy from a full-time instructional coach but also receive coaching from an assistant principal to help cultivate their leadership skills as a team lead. And sometimes this even shifts year over year. That same teacher might receive coaching from a literacy coach instead, for example. It reduces the risk of bias that is born from having a single person assigned to evaluate and cultivate your gifts. When you know that there are many people who might see your gifts, you are more likely to share them.

We have recurring structures of staff level-ups for a similar reason. A level-up is a meeting structure typical outside of the education sector, where employees have a routine opportunity to meet with the supervisor of their supervisor to provide feedback about their experience in the organization and the development they are receiving. The purpose is not intended to provide the employee with an opportunity to skirt the responsibility for giving direct feedback. That would undermine the trust and connection we seek to cultivate. To the contrary, a level-up should provide another mechanism to expand the organization's awareness of gifts. It is another opportunity to be seen.

A sense of safety is born from the knowledge that your needs will be met, that there is someone looking out for your best interests, someone standing with open arms, ready to embrace your gifts. The next challenge for a leader is the tough acknowledgment that not every action taken by a member of a school community presents immediately as a gift.

Welcome feedback as a gift.

In *Good to Great* Jim Collins discusses the qualities of a "Level 5 leader." These include an openness to people offering what may feel to the rest of us like out-of-the-box ideas.

Here is an example that is close to home. As I have illustrated through this book, the Jim Collins *Good to Great* idea of being "on the bus" is a core part of Brilla's identity. Collins used a bus to represent an organization with the leadership in the role of driver. The driver's job, Collins said, was to set the course and make sure the right people were on the bus to get it there.

It surprised us, then, when not long ago some members of staff pointed out that the image of the bus can evoke recollections of segregation. In our context especially, where the majority of students belong to minoritized ethnic groups, we do not take that lightly. Moreover, the image of the driver as "the boss" described a power dynamic antithetical to the partnership model we intend.

We had a lot invested in the phrase "on the bus," as you will have observed. It would have been easy to dismiss this feedback as an unwarranted criticism. But we remained open to it. After some thought, a change in this important phrase made sense to us. This feedback was indeed a gift: we are now "on the train," which is a more potent image, anyway, in a city where people are more likely to travel to school via subways than yellow buses. (As you will notice, we use the "on the train" analogy throughout the rest of this book.)

If Jim Collins should ever ask me, I would add that Level 5 leaders are those with the skill of being attentive to the dignity of the person standing in front of them. What a sad thing it would be for members of an organization if they did not feel the place where they went to work was led by people like that. They would not feel safe to be themselves. If the organization isn't open to their gifts, then why bother offering them?

In Brilla's early days we knew that realizing our vision would depend upon valuing, not merely tolerating, individual differences. It would mean lifting up the differences our kids, their families, and our staff bring to school, not smoothing them out or ignoring them.

Some gifts are comparatively easy to embrace, once you notice them. When someone observed that the inspirational quotes in our hallways were predominantly from white men, we moved quickly to add quotes from Maya Angelou, Barack Obama, Oscar Romero, and other leaders from diverse backgrounds. One year, staff indicated on a feedback survey that the absence of recess as part of our school day was limiting our ability to achieve the physical and social elements of our mission statement, so we adjusted the schedule. Other gifts are harder to embrace.

Seek input as a gift.

Ben Zoma said, "Who is wise? The one who learns from everyone."—Pirkei Avot 4:1

One day a staff member remarked that "Brilla is really good at asking for feedback but not so much at getting input." Naturally, it was a little hard to hear this (proving their point, I suppose).

We will pause here and define our terms. "Input" is a gift given before a decision is made. "Feedback" is an after-the-fact gift; it is still valuable but requires more effort to curb the momentum that has already taken form. Both are examples of people offering gifts. The tool that a leader has in pocket is to rely more heavily on input than on feedback. Here is a time when I learned that lesson the hard way.

In the first weeks of my first full year as principal, I had the great idea to eliminate the requirement of teachers to submit formal lesson plans for each of their guided reading groups. I had heard the feedback about how time-consuming they were to create, and I wanted to be responsive. Days into making that announcement, an email hit my inbox in the late afternoon. "Some of the teachers would like to meet with you after school. Please meet us in room 301 at 3:30."

You can imagine all the reactions that swam through my head. Some threatened to unhinge me: What had I done wrong? Was I about to experience a coup d'état? Were people about to quit? Others tested my humility: The nerve of demanding a meeting! And without context!

There was nothing to do other than show up. So I did, and I learned a few powerful leadership lessons. The first was about this concept of input.

What I learned from that meeting was that I had heard the feedback right, but I was wrong in my assessment of the root cause. Teachers did not want absolution from authoring lesson plans. They wanted a more efficient structure for collaborating to create a bank of them, and permission to do so. Though my action was inspired by feedback, it could have been shaped by input. And I had missed the opportunity. By not taking the time to engage with teachers about their ideas for how to improve the process for guided reading lesson plans, I had inadvertently created more problems than I started with. All of this could have been prevented if I had sought input as a gift.

The second lesson I learned from this situation was the power of responding to either feedback or input. It is not enough to seek it; it must be acted upon. That is not to say a leader must implement every suggestion they receive. That would be unreasonable and inefficient. But accepting all gifts requires us to truly listen when they are shared. To consider them openly and thoughtfully, and to express that we were listening in the way we respond.

In Step 2, I discussed the phenomenon of sending messages that for some reason are not received, or if they are received, they do not stick. Sometimes that is because of all the noise in our lives. But other times it is because what we have communicated is misperceived or misunderstood. A leader's responsibility is to clearly communicate the input or feedback that was received and how it has shaped (or not) the next steps that the organization will take. This critical step honors the heart that people expose when they share their gifts, and it also appeals to the rational mind by way of explanation. (Not to mention that it validates that someone actually reads all those surveys they are asked to complete.)

Welcoming input from everyone is not easy and requires ongoing effort, but it harnesses the collective genius of an organization. It wins the support of the people it depends upon to make the vision live. Thinking about inclusivity in this way flips the conversation from one that is defensive—"We'd better not screw this up"—to one that is alive to the rewards of multiple perspectives, all of them signed up for the same shared vision.

Embrace challenge as a gift.

Ironically, it is in the hard moments that a culture is strengthened, the moments when the culture's values are under stress. Not all of them are world historical moments like the COVID-19 crisis, but for the people involved they can feel just as consequential.

Sometimes in our schools, a student's promotion to the next grade is not a given. Sometimes it might be in the student's better interest to repeat a grade. Some schools are absolutist: meet the requirements for moving up or repeat the grade. Disenrolling, I suppose, is a third option.

Part of our commitment to making individuals feel safe inside our organization is the use of holistic data to inform the recommendation for advancement. If we have succeeded in winning a family's trust, we can talk candidly about the decision to promote a student.

We know this is a hard topic to talk about. We want families to feel safe if they need to cry, to talk about any stigma in the community, to think aloud about the impact on the family of having their child in school for an additional year. This is honoring their dignity.

Every conversation around this starts with the statement "We want your child to love school." Practice aligns with the stated commitment to partnership. The decision is the family's to make. Most families act on recommendations backed by evidence. They do so because we built the relationship, we built trust, and we have shown them that we mean it when we say they are the first educator. They believe us.

It is the same position we take when we teach reproductive education. In younger grades, that conversation is the families' to have. In middle school it is part of a unit on reproductive health. The first year we rolled this out, we announced it at one of our Parent University events. However, not every family was in attendance, so after the first day of instruction we were met with a number of angry phone calls from parents we had left unprepared to engage in follow-up conversations with their children and some who questioned our decision to teach it in the first place. Even a few who had heard our announcement were discontented with the preparation we provided. We learned from this blunder. We now actively partner with families to prepare for that curriculum and for the questions that might be coming their (and our) way. We explain the "why" of the curriculum both during Parent University and in written communications that all families receive. Instead of being an awkward moment, the effect is to uplift the dignity of the family at the center of a child's life. Families helped us learn how to make this part of the curriculum impactful. The culture was strengthened. Our seriousness about inclusivity was affirmed.

The parallels to the experience of staff are obvious. Exits are only one example, but a good one.

In most organizations, departures are a natural part of life. They happen throughout the year, usually with comparatively little drama attached. In a school, staff departures usually happen all at once at the end of term. This can create negative chatter. As I described in the last chapter, we work at making any decision to separate a process of mutual discernment and free choice.

When team members leave Brilla, they do so with grace. Going out in a ball of fire, leaving bridges burning behind you, does not serve the vision. The vision—serving our kids—is what we all signed up for. Add to this the relationships forged with colleagues and families who remain.

We manage any departure in ways that reflect our gratitude for the gifts individuals have offered our schools. First among these is the intentionality of our approach to communicating news about departures, which helps us get out ahead of any negative watercooler chatter by controlling the narrative.

Here's how it works. To begin, we believe that a departure is the staff member's story to tell. We work with departing staff so that people hear their story all at once—and in their own voice—rather than letting it leak out. Usually this happens at a specific MIP meeting in April, when transition news for the upcoming year (both departures and promotions) is shared. Staff honor our mutually beneficial approach by keeping their decision confidential prior to that time. During that MIP, they are cued when it is their moment to share. (Students are included in the messaging too, during a class meeting, so that familiar faces do not just disappear. Acting to the contrary would erode their trust in the adults who lead them.)

On the last day of school anyone leaving gets a proper sendoff. Team members who have worked with them prepare a toast to be given publicly. We wish them good fortune. We honor them as people, celebrating who they are as well as the contributions they made to our community. They have earned another star for their Boathouse jacket. We honor their gifts. We continue to convey an enduring sense of welcome even as they leave us.

The signals to those who remain are loud.

Getting it right is not always easy, whether with families or students or staff. What we intend by our actions is that our stakeholders will believe us when we say we tried to do the right thing. And that we are forever open to being better.

Several years ago we had a student who struggled with school nearly the whole time he was with us. Eventually his family moved away from the Bronx.

We were delighted when the following year the family came back to visit for our Mott Haven Celebration. It touched us that they still felt the pull of the connections they had formed, still felt drawn to participate in our culture. The student knew he was always welcome because while he was with us, even when he struggled, he felt respected. His mother proudly presented a note from his new teacher affirming how well he was doing at his new school, and she shared her gratitude for the partnership that had paved the way toward his current flourishing. We all knew he had gifts.

We had made a promise to that student. Keeping that promise needed more than good intentions. It needed serious attention to the details of execution, the subject to which I devote the final section of this book.

REFLECT ON YOUR PRACTICE

Extend a sincere welcome.
- How does your organization convey hospitality?
- How does each stakeholder group engage people who are not members of your school community?

Invite the whole person.
- What structured opportunities exist to invite members of your community to express deeper parts of themselves?

- What criteria do you use to guide planning or make decisions with specific awareness of their impact on the personal lives of those involved?

Make it safe to share gifts.

- How do you know if members of your school community feel safe to express ideas and parts of themselves without fear of repercussion, alienation, or silencing?

Welcome feedback as a gift.

- Does your organization actively seek and apply feedback?

- How does your organization respond when your initiatives are met with resistance or an alternative solution is proposed?

Seek input as a gift.

- Bearing in mind the distinction between input and feedback, what systems exist for pursuing input prior to implementing new initiatives or making changes, even in circumstances where time is limited?

Embrace challenge as a gift.

- What mindset do members of your organization bring to challenging situations?

- What challenges has your organization faced that brought new gifts to advance the organization?

PART 3

EXECUTION

STEP 7

Ensure Impact

Picture yourself planning a vacation. If you want to revel and relax in the comfort of the familiar, then it's easy. Just do what you've always done. Rebook. But if you are after a new memorable experience you need to put some effort into planning the details. And what you discover is that the anticipation this creates becomes a pleasurable part of the experience.[1] In your head you are on vacation before you are on vacation.

While you are away you try to make every moment count. That was the point of all the planning. If something you planned does not work out, you pivot and find a different way to spend your time. The whole time you are taking pictures, purchasing souvenirs, and maybe writing

---

[1] Jeroen Nawijn et al., "Vacationers Happier, but Most Not Happier after a Holiday," *Applied Research in Quality of Life* 5, no. 1 (2010): 35–47.

in a travel diary to make the sights and emotions of the experience stick more deeply in your memory. All of these elements enhance the impact of your vacation experience.

In the same way, and for just the same reasons, the work of a leader—building anticipation for an initiative, getting the details just right, being an active facilitator as the initiative is underway, sustaining the impact that everyone works so hard to achieve—cannot be left to chance.

Even the most routine meeting or policy rollout can be executed in a well-considered, well-managed, and—most importantly—well-remembered way. Doing it right is not a choice but a necessity, because doing it wrong is a net negative—people feel their time was wasted.

Execution is for nothing if the results do not stick. But when they do, they transform your practice and build commitment to your organizational vision.

HERE IS WHAT YOU ARE SIGNING UP FOR IN THIS CHAPTER.

* **Engineer anticipation.** When people are given opportunities to engage with an idea or an experience in advance, it piques their interest and amplifies the impact of the experience itself. There are countless ways of accomplishing this.
* **Sweat the details.** When we dream in detail the ways we want an event or a program initiative to serve the purposes of our vision, we can start to predict exactly what it will take to make it happen. It raises our odds of creating memorable experiences.
* **Actively manage.** Even something as familiar as a school dance should be treated as a risk-management moment. How we respond to the unexpected in real time reveals a great deal about how well prepared we were for when things go wrong. Even when things are going right, active management can elevate impact.

* **Sustain the impact.** Giving participants structured opportunities to reflect on an event creates the conditions for reliving it—not just in the immediate aftermath, but over time in ways that make your intentions durable.

* **Make the most of novelty.** If we want experience—any experience—to stay with us in a meaningful way, it needs an element to distinguish it from everything else vying for a place in our long-term memories. The most vivid experiences are those that participants can engage through multiple senses.

Engineer anticipation.

Every year in our schools we put a kid in a turkey costume. This student is sent around the halls to all the classrooms to hand out invitations to our annual Thanksgiving potluck for staff. The potluck, of course, is no surprise to anyone, since it is a tradition. Plus, by November it has been posted on our master calendar for months. But the tradition of a kid dressed up as a turkey boosts the event in just the ways we intend. The novelty of it in the midst of an otherwise predictable day, the delight at seeing which child was selected to wear the costume, and the anticipation it stimulates of gathering with colleagues to whom we feel connected spark positive feelings of connection, gratitude, and always some fresh joy, before the event even happens. It builds anticipation.

When people are given opportunities to engage with an idea in advance, it piques their interest. We can't help but to start imagining what we might experience. There are countless ways of accomplishing this once you begin thinking about it.

Think about this: in most organizations, performance reviews are not something assumed to stimulate positive anticipatory feelings in the person whose performance is being reviewed. That is not viewed as a review's purpose. Imagine changing that dynamic by asking staff

129

to complete a self-reflection prior to their review. What do they expect to hear? How would they assess their performance?

Feelings of anticipation would jump. Before the review formally begins conversation will have already started.

This approach underscores the conditions of participation by reminding us that a performance review does not need to be framed as something that is happening *to* us. It can be an opportunity to reflect on what we have signed up for, and whether we still wish to be on the train.

The experience is analogous to the difference between waiting in a line at Six Flags and in a line at Disneyland. Stay with me on this.

At Six Flags customers see only the long line in front of them. The best they can do is kill time and deal with their boredom until at last they get to the front. Queues at Disneyland, in contrast, are intentionally designed so that customers do not see much of the line ahead. They never really know how close to the front they are. But all along the way to their destination they see little teasers directly related to the ride they're anticipating. Instead of being bored, or at best indifferent, they are excited.[2] Even before the event they are creating a vision of the experience in their heads—an experience they have yet to actually have.

We wrap a birthday present for the same reason: it gives the receiver the pleasure of anticipation. Even before the gift is unwrapped, the receiver is invested in it, imagining what it might be. We should be doing the same with organizational initiatives.

Well before an event or the launch of an initiative—no matter what it is—we should be deliberately engineering the vibe we want to give participants, a vibe consciously derived from the organizational vision. It might be in the way an invitation is designed or an agenda is sent in advance. Perhaps there are clues or riddles to stimulate thinking,

---

[2] See, for example, Luis Perez Cortes and Kevin Close, "Designing Experience: A Case Study of Disneyland's Lines," *Talking About Design*, January 8, 2020.

or questions to consider. Maybe you build anticipation through spectacle, such as with the kids dressed as turkeys, an engaging iMovie, or a demonstration, whatever it may be. Making an initiative sticky requires an element that gets people hyped in advance, something that will add to a sense of shared experience before the event itself has properly begun. That is, something other than just dumping people in a room and hoping magic happens—because the odds are magic will not happen.

One year the philosopher Cornel West joined Brilla onboarding to give a presentation on what are often called "the transcendentals": truth, beauty, and goodness. Without naming who our guest would be, we sent around a snippet of his biography and asked people to guess. When we finally unveiled his name, we provided a link to a Google form that allowed people to submit questions. Just prior to the event we provided materials describing West's work. By the day of the speaking engagement, anticipation was sky-high.

Engineering anticipation will be familiar to good teachers. They talk about "hooks" all the time. Hooks are the tricks instructors use as a way of drawing students into a lesson. Hooks are also tools with which to seize an opportunity for creating pleasure in our work. A history teacher may come to school dressed as a historical character. A math teacher fills their classroom with the scent of sweet apple pie on Pi Day (March 14).

In planning anything, no matter what it is, actively look for hooks to amplify anticipation in service of greater impact. A good place to start is by asking yourself what you want attendees to later say about the event—what made it remarkable or important to them. Think about what you could do that would start to stimulate those reactions in advance.

If you can answer that question, you are halfway there.

Sweat the details.

The first time we put on a dance we forgot to ask ourselves what our intention was. So the day came, the music started, and the little kids just ran around. Which was fine, I guess, but not what we envisioned. We had hoped to give the kids an experience of something more meaningful. At a minimum, we had expected there to be actual dancing.

Our planning would have been more precise if we had asked ourselves better questions about what we intended. Lesson learned. Now we include teacher-led dance lessons (from "Cupid Shuffle" to "Y.M.C.A.") every time we host an elementary school party. That simple "what to do" transforms the experience for the kids.

Planning middle school dances is a different story. Middle schoolers don't run around. They hug the wall and stare at each other. So we designate a dedicated hype person to get the kids over their shyness and out on the dance floor. If our wider purpose is to help them build new relationships and to give them an experience they will remember, we need to be deliberate in anticipating what might get in the way of those outcomes and plan how to counteract them.

Sweating the details raises the odds of creating memorable experiences that yield the desired impact. What is your event or initiative going to look like if it is to serve your wider purpose—your vision? That question should inform the planning of every type of gathering.

Being that deliberate requires naming our intention out loud. If, for example, your intention is creating the conditions of connection, then having everyone come into an event and sit anywhere will, inevitably, lead to people sitting with people they already know. You may get some return in terms of small-group intimacy, but you miss the chance to create an experience that fosters new relationships that people will remember, tell others about, and recall gladly if they leave the organization.

This goes deeper than assigned seating. To make shared ownership for results more than an aspiration there needs to be some galvanizing element in the way people are brought together. Otherwise, organizers are left just hoping for the best. This is exactly the reason to plan on mixing up seating assignments—and "mix up" does not mean randomize.

Planners of an event generally know who is coming. The intention should be to seat people beside others with whom they do not normally have an opportunity to connect. It is also up to the planners to ensure that there is someone close by whom the attendees already know. That familiar person serves as an anchor, in a sense, encouraging individuals to feel comfortable—safe to share their gifts while engaging with someone new.

During the COVID-19 crisis we applied some of these lessons to planning virtual meetings. If we sent people into Zoom breakout groups, we were conscious of ways remote technologies can leave attendees feeling isolated and, therefore, reluctant to speak up. So we did two specific things to fight that tendency.

First, we were intentional in how we assigned individuals to breakouts, blending the well-acquainted with comparative strangers.

Second, we did not trust to natural chemistry to make the conversation flow. Someone was always the designated facilitator. Perhaps it was the person whose surname came first in the alphabet. The person charged with reporting for the group might be whoever's birthday came first in the year. Simple, but really effective in meaningfully increasing our odds of active participation.

In addition to considering how participants will engage with each other, also put thought into how they will engage with the content itself. For example, in professional gatherings most of us instinctively interact with new ideas by doing something physical, such as writing or typing. If there are transferable concepts to be captured for future use, what are the odds that everyone has conceived of a thoughtful method for doing so? I am guilty of vacillating between typing loose notes in a Word document, scribbling on the back of a handout, and snapping pictures of PowerPoint slides. It should not be so hard.

Instead, envision how people will store key takeaways as part of your planning efforts. Attach handouts to the calendar invite. Put the slide deck online in advance. Among other benefits, this practice smokes out presenters who throw together handouts at the last minute and then barely reference them during a session, or the ones who simply repurpose material developed for some other audience (it always shows).

In the old days we employed what we called "the book" during our onboarding events. The book was a binder that contained all the materials that would be used during onboarding, organized with tabbed sections and distributed to every staff member. All handouts were created in advance and put in the book. This was an upfront investment of time. In the long run it was a time-saver. During onboarding sessions there were no wasted minutes spent handing out materials. Our expectation was that throughout the year as handouts accumulated, they would live inside the book under the tabs where they belonged. If we are going for impact, the goal should not simply be that the resource material be stored or relegated to a single use. We want it to be perpetually referenced and applied.

If your goal is to ensure that participants will be able to absorb the message in the moment and then retrieve it in the future, sweat the details of how.

An organization can do all these things to plan strategically and might still be surprised by the unanticipated. To manage risks arising from the unexpected, you and your stakeholders need to actively manage your initiatives in real time.

Actively manage.

You may have noticed that life is full of surprises, not all of them good. This is true even when we think we have made all the right moves.

One year, for instance, the marketing for our school's Costume Carnival event was a huge success. That was the bad news. The line out the door went so far back that families were beginning to take their children home. Inside the school our plan for having everyone progress from one numbered booth to the next was stymied by the tendency of little kids to find an activity they like and stick with it. We planned the event to provide a positive experience for families to make memories as a school community. Instead people were leaving with a sour taste. On the spot we realized we had to open a second entry door and forget the sequencing of booths.

In our planning meetings for that carnival, the question "What if the line is really long?" had never come up. Afterward we were left with even more useful questions. Did our culture encourage us to be proactive? When called upon to be reactive, how did we adapt ourselves? If our culture is durable, it should enable us to respond vigorously to the unanticipated, even when we have done good planning—not just in the case of a carnival, but in larger moments too.

We learned in real time that dealing with something as seemingly basic as the line at a carnival was a risk management moment, one that revealed a great deal about how well prepared we were for when things go wrong.

Do not assume that because you have made a detailed plan, an initiative will go off well. Part of any planning process has to include someone—perhaps multiple people—to monitor events in real time. It is not antithetical to mutual accountability and distributed leadership to give someone the task of supervision. These are activists on behalf of the vision—hype people of a different kind, maybe, but similar in purpose to the ones at our dances.

You might, for example, plan a solid professional development event, and then, to your astonishment, participants are silent. Do not let that go. Instead, in your plan provide for two or three individuals ready with a couple of pump-priming questions if a group is too quiet. Cause conversation to happen.

Rapid feedback ought to be a through line of your planning. Good teachers, for instance, do not wait until the day of an exam to find out whether students are meeting learning objectives. They are collecting performance data all the time and acting on it. The same is true for event planning and follow-through. Do not wait until an event is over to see how it went. By then it will be too late to adjust the plan.

When we do our annual Thanksgiving potluck, we intend the occasion to encourage expressions of gratitude among colleagues. We sweat the details. We build in time for writing notes to one another, even providing paper of a particular size so that everyone has a gauge of expected length. We provide parameters: two notes to one's immediate team, another to someone on the leadership team, another to someone on the operations team, and so on.

While staff is writing, the hosts are collecting the notes and depositing them in jars with the name of each guest. They monitor the jars to make sure everyone is getting notes. If we are striving for everyone's gifts to be accepted, how can we allow the chance that someone might be overlooked? (It happened once, which is how we learned this lesson.) If necessary, leaders will write a note themselves, or nudge one of the attendees to write one.

This kind of granular attention in real time should be typical. This is not an instance of micromanaging. It is an illustration of using the active management of a school initiative, be it a meeting, event, development session, or other, to ensure execution that meets the goal.

The work a school does every day to build a culture committed to shared vision sets a tone for how to act during moments of challenge. A healthy culture should empower people to solve problems when they happen. If our relationships have substance, we will be less inclined to hand off a problem to someone else. We want the show to go on. Succeeding becomes personal and relational.

Sustain the impact.

We have all had the experience of sitting in a professional event thinking, "This is great. I can't wait to get back to work and apply this." Then life moves along, and the vividness of the moment begins to fade. We find ourselves back in the grind, the outcome of our participation being inspiration maybe, but not impact. How can we recall those feelings and return them to front and center?

The word "memory" comes from a Latin word that means "to fix in the mind." Everyone wants a professional development event to be memorable in that way. Everyone wants the school dance they hosted to be recalled years later and associated with the wider purpose behind it. Assuming you manage to pull that off, how will you sustain the impact you made?

Be guided by two words: reflect and relive. Reflect by giving participants opportunity to think back on an event and the feelings or learning associated with it. You might do this with journal writing or by sharing highlights. Relive by creating an experience that allows stakeholders to revisit their experience. This is not a suggestion to literally recreate an experience. Rather, it is to artfully recollect specific memories associated with the original experience.

Well-considered efforts at recollection (from the Latin "recolligere," to take up again, or regain) yield a double benefit: a deeper connection to the vision and the school community, and a greater likelihood of a yes when staff are asked on the Gallup Q^{12} whether they have had opportunities to learn and grow in their work. It will be one more thing they can write about on their performance review self-assessment.

Create opportunities for stakeholders to reminisce and share stories about specific details from an event. You might plan a subsequent staff meeting prompt in which attendees are paired up and invited to discuss takeaways from the event, such as "How will we apply the new ideas this week?" Then perhaps a week later, reinforce the condition of mutual accountability by having the pairs regroup and discuss how well the ideas worked in application.

How much more powerful—and enduring—that would be than if the last word ever heard about an experience was the presenter saying, "Thanks for coming. Hope you learned something."

Another method is to use digital media to highlight specific details from an event. Videos, photographs, and almost any other mementos work. They can be printed or included in an email, on a display, or in a slideshow.

Throughout the year we bring everyone together for slide shows that remind us of work we have done together and of the moments we have shared. Immediately after events we post photos on the staff fridge and on social media. Photographs help us tell the story of our culture by evoking memories of what we have shared.

For elementary school students still learning to read, pictures are audience-appropriate—and they can be impactful for adults as well. At our staff onboarding, which is only a two-week experience, we take pictures. They cue us to reflect and relive. They help all of us recall what we accomplished together even before we meet the students. They underline what was sticky about our shared experiences. They evoke the energy of our vision at its most tactile.

Reliving an experience is, in a sense, the bookend to building anticipation. All over again our hearts and minds are activated, we become inspired, and we are renewed in our commitment to being on the train.

Make the most of novelty.

We all love traditions. But the same old same old does not cue the release of adrenaline. Brain science tells us that human beings are wired to remember anything that feels new.[3] If we want experience to give us something memorable, that is to say, something with enduring impact, then it needs constant refreshment.

Several years ago a pair of neuroscientists, Nico Bunzeck and Emrah Düzel, used magnetic resonance imagery to observe the reaction of the brain to novelty. Here's what they found: when confronted with something new, the part of our brain that governs responses to rewards and helps shape our behaviors lights up. It turns out our

---

[3] D. Ramirez Butavand et al., "Novelty Improves the Formation and Persistence of Memory in a Naturalistic School Scenario," *Frontiers in Psychology* 11 (January 29, 2020).

brains physically crave novelty. Novelty affects our brains in ways that amplify our sense of fulfilment.[4]

When I was in fifth grade my teacher was Ms. Enayati. She was the sort of teacher who gave kids the feeling of being in Ms. Frizzle's class.[5] Everything felt new, never canned. The process of learning was not rote and robotic. It was perpetually stimulating—we felt like we were getting away with something. In her classroom there was always novelty.

One of Ms. Enayati's jobs, for instance, was to oversee our school's internal TV network. Inevitably, her class did the lion's share of work on broadcasts to the rest of the school. We sharpened our writing skills in the process, alongside our collaborative skills and research skills— fulfilling fifth grade learning standards without ever realizing it.

My sixth grade science teacher, Ms. Clymer, had us investigate different forms of energy. She encouraged us to tell the story of what we learned however we liked, as long as it was accurate. My friend and I were assigned wind. We made a music video scored to a Mariah Carey song that was all about wind power. Even today I can cite random facts about wind energy.

My encyclopedic knowledge of wind power sticks because I acquired it through novelty. Novelty gave me delight. Delight produced engagement. Engagement produced enduring impact.

Novelty draws us into an experience. It makes the familiar new again.

As I described in Step 3, "Signal Shared Identity," traditions are essential tools for binding a community. But traditions should never be an excuse for autopilot. If traditions are not balanced with new experiences, the hold they have over us will grow weak and eventually wane.

---

[4] See, for example, Joachim Morrens et al., "Cue-Evoked Dopamine Promotes Conditioned Responding during Learning," *Neuron 106*, no. 1 (February 5, 2020): 142–153.

[5] Ms. Frizzle is a fictional teacher from the popular children's series *The Magic School Bus*, who inspired love of learning in her students by exposing them to concepts during fantasy-based field trips

We could, for example, get our Thanksgiving potluck catered. The food would be good, and the first time we did it, I'm sure people would remember. But a few years in, it would become trite. If our intention is not to create a memorable experience, but simply to break bread together, that would be fine. And to be fair, sometimes it is. (Novelty overdone can be problematic in its own ways.) But for us, the potluck represents a very intentionally crafted large group moment for connection. We want to turn what could be an ordinary gathering into something memorable. Thinking about what food item to contribute, and then cooking it in advance, fosters anticipation. Participants come to the event already engaged. While there, they have a built-in conversation topic: "What food item did you bring?" Afterward, our method for sustaining impact can be to circulate a recipe book of what was shared. It really all does come back to your intention.

Novelty can be simple, like changing the décor of the physical space where we hold our potluck. We once created a memorable professional development event that focused on the classical virtues by having our founding board chair appear in a toga. To this day no one has forgotten about that one.

Human brains have evolved to crave what we can see, touch, hear, feel, and taste. So make what you do as tactile as you can. That is how we make sense of the world in the most durable way.

In this chapter I have offered what might seem humble examples of planning and follow-through: a potluck, a school dance, a professional development session. If you are building a culture that intends to win hearts and minds, these are not so humble examples. The purpose of each of these initiatives is to realize your vision of high performance. So, any step you can take to maximize impact as you execute is worth the investment. Fortunately, there are other tools of execution to drive results, specifically time and treasure.

••

REFLECT ON YOUR PRACTICE

Engineer anticipation.

- What opportunities are stakeholders given to engage with content in advance of experiencing it?

- What do you do to ensure early exposure to an event or a professional program to pique the interest of participants in advance?

Sweat the details.

- In your planning for an event or for a new program, what measures are in place to ensure that every element of your vision is maximized for successful implementation?

- What methods do you employ to anticipate pitfalls, misconceptions, and surprises in advance of an event or a program rollout?

Actively manage.

- Once a program or an event goes live, how is the responsibility for its success distributed?

- What strategies do hosts or facilitators employ to monitor your program or event to ensure that all the elements of your vision are visible in the effort?

Sustain the impact.

- Once a program or school event is complete, what steps do you take to sustain its success?

- What do you do that enables participants to relive positive feelings from an event or to reflect and act upon insights gleaned from programming?

Make the most of novelty.

- What elements do you employ to make an initiative memorable?

- What about your programming stimulates the senses in a manner that is unique?

- How have you applied novel elements to traditions to ensure continued engagement?

STEP 8

Ledger Time and Treasure

Most people probably don't know that when the United States decided to go to the moon in less than nine years, most of the country was not at all sold on the idea. The vision was too large, people said, the money was better spent on other needs. In 1964, three years into the moon program, only 26 percent of Americans thought the effort was worthwhile. Norbert Wiener, one of the most prominent mathematicians in the world at the time, famously called the Apollo project a "moondoggle."

And still it happened.

This book has taken inspiration from the story of the custodian at Cape Canaveral who considered himself an integral participant in the great adventure of landing on the moon. The point to remember about that story is that the custodian would never have felt that way if he believed his time and money were being wasted.[1]

Leaders in large corporations are familiar with the term "resource alignment." The idea is that how we use time and allocate money and other organizational resources (aka "treasure") needs to be consistent with our declared strategic goals. To ledger time and treasure is to collect data about the ways an organization deploys its finite resources of time and money, and other forms of treasure such as rewards and recognition, and audit the data collected against the stated goals of the vision. Whether our vision is to assert world leadership by landing an astronaut on the moon or to promote the holistic development of children, our vision needs to show up in the ways we budget our time, spend our money, and reward or recognize what we value.

Calendar and budget may be the two hard resources over which school leadership has the most direct influence. Organizations should be auditing both all the time for data to ensure that the ways they allocate time and money reflect who they say they are and what they want to achieve. The concept of treasure, however, can be extended beyond money. Especially for leaders, the ability to decide what to reward and recognize in the school community is a form of treasure that carries immense value among its people. In fact, recent research suggests that praise is more valuable than money as a motivating force for fulfilling your vision.[2] It follows that leaders should also audit who and what they celebrate or convey gratitude for to gauge its alignment with what the vision claims to value.

The powerful thing about hard data is that they are just facts. Data are not emotional (although our interpretations of data can be). Used correctly, data tell a story the same way an X-ray tells a story to a doctor studying it.

---

[1] Charles Fishman, "What You Didn't Know about the Apollo 11 Mission," *Smithsonian Magazine*, June 2019.

[2] Richard Eisenberg, "What Workers Crave More Than Money," Forbes.com, September 27, 2016.

The impact of strategically allocating limited resources—like the consequences of getting it wrong—are measurable. Collected data allow school leadership to set targets and judge how close they are to hitting them in real time. In a healthy school culture, the information gathered from ledgering time and treasure need not be a scary thing at all. On the contrary, we should be grateful for the intelligence it provides.

HERE IS WHAT YOU ARE SIGNING UP FOR IN THIS CHAPTER:

✳ **Master the calendar.** The creation of a single master calendar allows the whole school community to see where time is being spent in ways that spotlight synergies and conflicts with the expressed aspirations of the vision.

✳ **Cascade from the macro to the micro.** Consciously working from the large goals of the school vision to the most granular expenditures of time ensures that the alignment of every hour of the school day is intended as support for what we have all signed up for.

✳ **Measure your treasure.** People in organizations notice the way money is spent. They are quick to spot gaps between the allocation of cash and what the school claims to value. Put your money where your priorities are.

✳ **Recognize what you value.** Money alone is an impoverished way of defining treasure. It would be a mistake to think that money is the single measure of value in any organization, but in schools most of all. What leaders choose to express gratitude for and what they choose to celebrate are both powerful forms of treasure. Consciously allocate all forms of treasure in alignment with your vision.

Master the calendar.

Here is a universal truth: time is a finite resource.[3] We cannot make more of it. How we spend time matters intensely. Time should be as tangible to an organization's leadership as money in the bank. Your district might define large elements of your calendar. And still you have authority over how your time is spent.

For all my faith in distributed leadership the one job I will never give up is calendaring. My team needles me about this all the time. "You should delegate that," they say. "It's too trivial for your role." To me nothing could be more strategic than time management. How we organize time tells everything about what we believe to be our priorities.

Another way to put it is that calendaring is our way of ensuring that we begin with the end in mind. Then, capturing the data from our experience that can tell us whether we have reached our intention.

We keep our master calendar in Excel. From time to time (that is not a pun) I have been urged to switch to an ordinary Google calendar. But a Google calendar simply captures when things are scheduled to happen and who will attend. It is an insufficient portrait of our priorities. Useful, but not strategic.

If we are going to be strategic about deploying time as a structural support for our vision, then we need a map across the year—not just the conventional school year but the whole year. We need to see a single event in its relation to other single events in multiple domains— to ensure, for example, that we do not have community-building events and academic events fighting each other for priority. We need to be able to observe how events ebb and flow with each other so that they do not become overwhelming to plan and participate in. The master calendar, a document that shows how time is allocated on a daily, weekly, and

---

[3] Except maybe in the quantum universe. See, for example, Natalie Wolchover, "Does Time Really Flow? New Clues Come from a Century-Old Approach to Math," Quanta Magazine, April 7, 2020.

monthly basis across each critical element of our vision, is our tool for finding balance among the different pieces of our vision.

Think of the master calendar as a ledger tallying whether the things you spend your time on support your vision. At Brilla, we build the master calendar backward from the goal of developing staff practice. That way we can have higher confidence that annual, weekly, and daily schedules are balanced in pursuit of each element of our vision.

We manage the building of our master calendar in waves. First come the nonnegotiables—first day of school, last day of school, holidays, vacations. With those nailed down we begin the work of asking ourselves whether the way we structure time—the way we spend time—encourages not just academic achievement but virtue formation, community building, and all the other elements of the vision for our school that we intend to realize.

A master calendar, for example, makes it immediately clear what a huge mistake it would be if the high points in our year were limited exclusively to activities that generate academic achievement. Were that the case, it would signal that academics was the sole portion of our vision we prioritize, whatever we say to the contrary.

We develop our master calendar with input from all directions. If we were to ask our academics department to set the calendar for assessments while simultaneously asking the culture lead to plan parent events, we would end up with the kind of unbalanced time budget we work to avoid. By collaborating on building the master calendar, we have global insight into the organization's time management and can avoid misapplications of time or inadvertent overlaps—we might see that a December door decorating competition, for example, is scheduled in the same week as family conferences. It might sound like a good idea to bring parents in when all the decorations are up, but for a teacher it is a stress nightmare. They cannot uphold both as priorities at the same time and do either well.

So, which item is the priority, and which one is going to play second fiddle? Whichever it is, people will notice.

Something like this might seem like a small thing in the life of a school. Trust me, it is not. Anyone who has worked in a school has had the experience of an overfull plate of scheduled deliverables that compete with what they thought they had signed up for: teaching kids.

For another example, the logical time for midyear staff performance reviews is March. But March also happens to be the height of test prep for New York State exams. Seeing the two crowding one another on the master calendar alerted us that conducting performance reviews in March would likely pit these priorities against each other.

We even calendar when we will collect key data points throughout the year. For example, we capture culture-building data in all kinds of ways, never forgetting that what we choose to measure tells everything about what the organization values. We do not, for example, choose one day or one week when we capture all the data points that matter. As accountants say, that would be just a snapshot in time. Throughout the year we measure staff performance against progress to our goals, not just in an annual performance review. For example, we apply Gallup's Q^{12} tool to measure staff engagement in October and June.

Just by creating a master calendar we demonstrate our intention of balancing the essential elements in our vision. It can shine a spotlight on the ways time is spent that might be misaligned with your vision. Then you can begin to make a fix.

Cascade from the macro to the micro.

Some might argue that a school calendar is mostly plug and play—that once you have built it out you can simply replicate it with the correct dates for the following year. They could not be more wrong. It would be malpractice to produce a financial budget that way. The same is true of a calendar.

We scrutinize the master calendar the same way we scrutinize our financial budget. We need to be sure the components of our vision are captured for the human beings who make our vision live. We need to ensure we are applying lessons learned from living the calendar during the previous year and adapting to any contextual changes driven by the education sector at large.

The master calendar as we have designed it cascades from the macro to the micro. Here is an example of what I mean.

Roughly every six weeks we schedule a Mission in Progress session dedicated to character formation. There is a strategic rationale for this investment of time: we cannot nourish in students what we do not have in ourselves. That would be like employing a math teacher trained in pedagogy who did not know arithmetic. Yet when we started introducing character to our vision, our expenditure was only twenty minutes per session. Now each session is forty-five minutes long. The heavier investment of time is a loud and recurring signal of what the organization values. We took a piece of our macro vision—character formation—and manifested it at the micro level of the master calendar.

I could cite a long list of things that should appear on a master calendar. It would include time for collecting student achievement data across all subjects, including tests and performance assessments. It would also include the collection of character data I described in the "Vision" section of this book. And it would include student enrollment, attendance, staff retention, staff performance, and Q^{12} data. In terms of programming, the master calendar would indicate not only staff MIPs but also a schedule for family conferences; events for students, staff, and families; and other vision-driven programming, ranging from picture day for students to onboarding for staff. Successful outcomes for all of these are a function of the time invested in making them happen.

Attention to the way staff spend time inevitably leads to reflections on how that flows into the next closest circle of influence—our students—and through students to families.

During the school day we promote character formation for our kids. Where on the calendar are things we do with and for families? We say community building is as central to our vision as virtue formation. Shouldn't it be manifest in the planning of family events?

It should, and it is.

In too many schools, community-building events are jammed at the end of the year. Field days, dress-down days, talent shows—all these things get scheduled for the weeks before school ends. The implicit signal to the community is that compared to work in the classroom, these events are of lower priority. And besides, by June everyone is exhausted anyway.

We intentionally take the opposite approach. As we do with other parts of our calendar, we work backward, beginning at the macro level. We frontload several of our marquee community-building events. Then we make sure the master calendar has the rest of them happening throughout the year at a strategic pace. Often we schedule these for the Friday before an extended break or long weekend, giving everyone something to look forward to and show up for when they might otherwise be inclined to start their vacations early (physically or mentally).

In the fall, not too long after returning to school, we schedule a big event for families and staff, our Mott Haven Celebration. We do another in March when the weather begins to improve, and then another in June. Then there are the Parent Universities regularly scheduled throughout the school year, strategically interspersed between community events. These are another instance of building a master calendar that cascades from the macro—delivering on the school's vision—to the micro detail of a specific block of hours on a specific Saturday.

All year long we seek feedback on how we can better align our time and schedules to execute our vision. We use this data to reboot the master calendar annually. Every Friday, for example, each grade team runs a looking-back protocol in their team meeting in which they ask themselves, "OK, what happened this week that we can do better? Are there takeaways we want to capture that can inform the way we calendar our priorities for next year?" Manufacturing companies do the same thing with continuous-improvement processes. In that way the impact of their work cascades over time.

We do not always get the balance right. There was a time when we did not schedule time for recess, for instance. Perhaps without admitting it to ourselves, we viewed recess as time taken from the pursuit of higher academic achievement. I know there are resources supporting the proposition that if you get kids moving, it does positive things for student academic performance.[4] If we scheduled recess for that reason, we would still be manifesting academic achievement as the goal beyond every other. Anyway, in the short-term recess might not lead to higher academic achievement. And we might have to be OK with that.

Above any of these rationales, the word "physical" is part of our vision. Seeing our kids active and taking care of their bodies is as valued in our vision as learning to read. The way we spend time needs to reflect that.

Everyone on our train knows this. We tell them so all the time. The master calendar helps uncover gaps in our execution against these goals. It not only captures how different mission-critical elements are prioritized, but when we will collect data about each of those elements. And once again we do it by beginning with the end in mind, exactly as we do with the way we spend money.

Measure your treasure.

Say we were to give each staff member a $200 gift card during the winter holidays. That would feel good, especially since it puts a high value on financial rewards. But what if instead $40 was spent on a team dinner that built relationships? And another $60 was used to buy swag customized to that team. Then perhaps $100 personalized to an individual staff member's specific interest—tickets to a sporting event for one, credit at a specialty store for another. The net effect of communicating value to the employee would remain, but in addition we would see a return on other core elements that drive culture in pursuit of our

---

[4] Vickie Beard, "A Study of the Purpose and Value of Recess in Elementary Schools as Perceived by Teachers and Administrators," doctoral dissertation, Eastern Tennessee School of Graduate Studies, August 2018.

vision: creating connection, signaling shared identity, and accepting people's gifts by celebrating them in an individualized way.

Which is the better investment of $200?

You must spend your monetary treasure wisely. When it comes to circles of influence, money is the element over which leadership might seem to have the most direct control.

We cannot make more time but, theoretically, we can make more money. Except, of course, when access to money is constrained by the state in which one operates. That does not change the fact people in organizations notice the way money is spent every bit as much as they do time.

If we want to create opportunities to build relationships and reinforce our shared identity, we back that up with budget for dinners together, decorations to make staff events memorable, tickets for bonding activities, and swag.

If we want to use physical space to communicate a vision of welcome, we back that up with budget for warm lighting, signs pointing visitors where to go, and clean floors.

If we declare that the staff lounge will be an inviting place for professionals to connect and recharge, we back that up with budget for couches and coffee.

These are relatively low-cost considerations. An effective fiscal steward can find ways to make ideas like these happen. But there are high-cost considerations, as well, where leadership must be the ones to step up and put our money where our vision is.

Brilla schools, for instance, have always employed instructional coaches for literacy and instructional coaches for math. For character development, all the instructional coaches were teacher leaders. But a teacher's first job is teaching. Promoting the character component of our program was always going to come second for a teacher-leader. We declared that character was equal in importance to math and literacy, and yet there was no one at the campus level working on it full time.

(What should the organization conclude from that?) So we hired full time character initiatives leads.

To give another example, part of our vision states that an effective teacher is a prize among our talent landscape. Yet many of our best teachers were leaving the classroom for the higher salaries awarded to instructional coaches. So, we found budget for a master teacher stipend—serious money. Now a master teacher can make more money than if they were to pursue a promotion to become an instructional coach.

What we spend treasure on signals what we value and what we do not, what we celebrate and what we don't.

There is probably no area where organizations notice how money is spent more than with respect to compensation. If we say we honor individual dignity, then we need to pay staff members properly. If we claim we value teachers, that needs to show up in salaries.

Looking at a school's financial budget should provide data on more than just where the money goes. It should provide data on where the school makes investments in its vision and where it falls short.

In our annual state of the schools presentation, we put up a pie chart of how our budget is spent. By being this transparent, staff can see that more than half our budget goes to compensation. They are also reminded of many of the fixed expenses that limit our ability to allocate money elsewhere, including rent, maintenance costs, materials and supplies.

People understand compensation as a measure of how much they are valued in their jobs. As many schools do, we place value on years of experience. The wisdom gleaned from experience aligns with our core virtue. The other primary driver of compensation is effectiveness, derived explicitly from our performance reviews. This illustrates another reason why we need to be incredibly intentional in ensuring that we are measuring what matters in designing these reviews. Were our teacher reviews to focus exclusively on classroom management and character building, that would be a clear message, but the wrong one. Teachers who expertly guide students toward higher academic achievement might wonder how much it really mattered.

Recognize what you value.

For most of us, compensation is not the only reward that motivates us. There is ample research showing that people amplify commitment to their jobs when they feel recognized. In schools, recognition most often comes in the form of expressions of gratitude (recognition through words) or explicit celebrations (recognition through gifts or experiences).

In an experiment described in the *Journal of Personality & Social Psychology,*[5] participants kept records of their moods and coping behaviors in response to a variety of life situations. One group was asked to note what they did to control their situations. Another group was asked to describe what they felt gratitude for. People in a third group were randomly assigned to either the control condition or the gratitude condition.

Results suggest that a conscious focus on gratitude may have emotional and interpersonal benefits. People at Brilla, from kindergartners to custodial staff, will back that up. That is the reason we create traditions of gratitude to signal its essential role in our vision. We let people know that we treasure them and their contributions to our vision, and we provide time and resources to enable them to show that same appreciation to others.

One example would be the way that we recognize and celebrate employees of the month. First, they are nominated and voted on by staff. It is a condition of participation. We then budget money—and time—for celebrating the honoree. But neither the time nor the money is prescribed. The methods of celebration are intended to be inspired by the five love languages, as described by author Gary Chapman in

---

[5] Robert A. Emmons and Michael E. McCullough, "Counting Blessings versus Burdens: An Experimental Investigation of Gratitude and Subjective Well-Being in Daily Life," *Journal of Personality and Social Psychology* 84, no. 2 (2003): 377–389.

his book, *The Five Love Languages: The Secret to Love that Lasts.* This text has been influential to Brilla in its affirmation that people feel love and appreciation in different ways. Expressing our gratitude for their gifts with a simple financial reward would suffice only for those who feel love in that way. In fact, the trend in the research about the modern workplace goes firmly against money as the primary motivator, with 70 percent of survey respondents reporting that their most meaningful recognition "had no dollar value."[6]

To ensure that our gratitude efforts have an impact among those who sense love through words of affirmation, we create a video of students, colleagues, and members of their families expressing gratitude for the honoree. For those who are most uplifted by acts of service, their fellow staff members may volunteer to run copies for them, undertake the labor of updating a bulletin board, or cover a class so that the honoree can leave early one day.

As a ledger of treasure, reflecting on the various ways in which we show gratitude– in both prescribed and non-prescribed moments—will win hearts and have a direct effect on outcomes. The process need not be burdensome. Intentional structures like a shout-out board in the staff lounge or shout-outs written into a newsletter help provide a structural support to influence the desired action. (However, given the often free-form nature of these, be mindful that they do not undermine your vision by becoming unbalanced in who they spotlight or what elements are emphasized.) Having staff or students complete a survey indicating how they most feel love or gratitude, supported with details, can take the guesswork out of choosing your method. Having a bin of treats like snack bars, chips, or sweets available on demand eliminates time needed to shop or order. The influencer strategy of modifying the environment (designating a shout-out board, having treats on hand) can be leveraged to cultivate a culture of gratitude.

---

[6] Victor Lipman, "Employee Study Shows Recognition Matters More Than Money," *Psychology Today,* June 13, 2013.

Value is conveyed not only in what we choose to recognize or express gratitude for, but also in what we choose to celebrate or reward. Think about the things your school celebrates. Are those celebrations core to your vision? Are they in balance across the school year?

Central to our school's identity is celebrating both growth and achievement in our scholars. We host a weekly celebrations block as part of the Friday schedule that provides an explicit opportunity to recognize growth and achievement in both academics and virtue.

Approximately monthly, our grades assemble in the Nest to celebrate talents in the school community. That might mean a spelling bee, a fine and applied arts showcase, or a talent show. It might mean participation in our mock version of the Winter Olympic Games or spring field day. These activities are not meant to emphasize competition. Though some of these do take on that format (and others intentionally do not), the priority is to conduct them in an atmosphere of celebration and recognition for the gifts that each of us brings across different elements of our vision. Ledger what you celebrate, and how often, to ensure that all elements that are core to your vision are appropriately recognized.

The way an organization spends its time and treasure must align with the claims it makes for its vision. It should be structured in a manner that is operationally coherent—which is to say intentional. Having a ledger for both time and treasure keeps track of what has been invested and what the return has been. Return on the investment is measured by growth—growth in terms defined by the vision and by the outcomes produced by the people on the train. The people, as we have discussed previously, are the core driver of your school's success.

REFLECT ON YOUR PRACTICE

Master the calendar.
- How do the ways your school allocates time (for staff, students, and families) align with the values of your vision?
- How do you assess the impact of time allocations in service of your vision—your return on investment?

Cascade from the macro to the micro.
- How are your school's annual, weekly, and daily schedules aligned in support of your vision?
- How does your calendar ensure data will be collected across all elements of your vision?

Measure your treasure.
- How do the ways your school allocates fiscal resources align with the values of your vision? (Consider materials, development, staffing, compensation, etc.)
- How do you assess the impact of financial expenditures in service of your vision—your return on investment?

Recognize what you value.
- How do the ways your school demonstrates gratitude for stakeholder contributions align with the values of your vision?
- How do your school celebrations align with the values of your vision?
- How do you assess the impact of expressions of gratitude and celebrations in service of your vision—your return on investment?

STEP 9

Keep Courting Talent

Here is something I know from experience: when the work is hard, the best sorts of people show up. And when you get them truly bought in for the long haul, the sky is the limit.

Herman Aguinis and Ernest O'Boyle Jr., in their rigorous "study of studies" for *Personnel Psychology*[1] in 2012, challenged a long-held assumption in talent management circles that individual performance in organizations will, over time, cluster around a mean. In their study of more than 600,000 researchers, entertainers, politicians, and athletes, Aguinis and O'Boyle found that high-performers are 400 percent more productive than the average. According to Aguinis and O'Boyle, the gap

---

[1] Herman Aguinis and Ernest O'Boyle Jr., "The Best and the Rest: Revisiting the Norm of Normality in Individual Performance," *Personal Psychology* 65, no. 1 (2012); cited in Scott Keller and Mary Meaney, Leading Organizations: Ten Timeless Truths (Bloomsbury Publishing, 2017).

between the best and the rest rises with a job's complexity. In complex occupations, high performers are 800 percent more productive than the mean. Any educator can attest to the complexity of leading a classroom of thirty unique individuals who have not yet developed all of their mental, social, and emotional capacities. Imagine the outcomes we could achieve for kids if we could attract these high performers to our schools and win the buy-in of their hearts and minds.

No vision of great richness can be realized without the right people—not merely good people but the right people. When anyone in any occupation feels love for their work, their job becomes a vocation. When your job is your vocation, your expectation is that your work has no start or stop time, no boundary of responsibility. If I am great at what I do—not merely skilled but committed—I come into work in the morning understanding what my mission is. I'm hungry for it. I come to work with a conviction that the organization is mine to take care of.

That is what gives meaning to the life of a high performer.

Don't assume that once great people have come aboard your train that you have them hooked. As you may have heard, honeymoons end. We have to keep courting talent.

I use the term "talent" broadly, as all organizations should. My definition embraces people working in the classroom, of course, but it also equally includes operational staff, administrative staff, and frankly anyone working in a school building. Recall that you can't make anyone do anything. Staff members have free choice to give their minds and hearts to the work or not, to either continue on the train or step off.

Families and students are no different. They are the talent that drives the vision for the train in the first place. And they also have free choice. Our existence is dependent upon families leveraging their free choice to choose our schools. Without winning the hearts and minds of families, there are no students to teach, no fiscal resources to work from, no purpose to our work. And certainly no high performance.

Everyone matters in getting the train where it's going. In terms of execution, talent is the most valuable resource.

The first question any leadership team must ask itself, then, is this: who is the ideal talent for realizing the vision?

The second question is, where do we find such people?

The third is, how do we keep them?

HERE IS WHAT YOU ARE SIGNING UP FOR IN THIS CHAPTER:

* **Recruit for the vision.** Even in an age of talent shortages, there are lots of gifted people in the world. A successful recruiting strategy will be a search for talent as committed to your school's vision as you are.

* **Select for the vision.** Use the time *before* new talent joins your organization as a prime opportunity for all parties to be clear on what they are signing up for.

* **Keep them warm.** Do not treat the time between a commitment to membership and formally initiating membership as a blank space. Fill it with opportunities to invest in the school's vision.

* **Onboard for commitment.** Onboarding as it is practiced in most schools is all about training and orientation. It should be a full immersion in the vision and in all the steps required to make the vision come to life.

* **Coach constantly.** Good coaching is strength based and, even more importantly, ongoing. Never miss an opportunity to reinforce and affirm when talent is uplifting the vision. Be intentional and timely when redirection is required, because talent is taking action that undermines the vision.

* **Evaluate against the vision.** View evaluation as a formal stamp of an ongoing coaching conversation that ensures responsiveness to the vision holistically.

Recruit staff for the vision.

Many readers of this book are probably familiar with what is known as the warm-body phenomenon. It refers to the panic some schools feel at the idea of a staff vacancy. Panic fuels the impulse to simply fill the position as quickly as possible, as if anyone will do. Setting aside any conversation about basic skills, if a warm body is not aligned with the vision, they can do more damage than a temporarily open position ever could.

If a new hire is aligned with the vision, execution is likely to follow. Corporate recruiters call this fit. Recruiting for the vision needs to be a deliberate, patient process. An organization in recruitment mode must do a lot more than cast a net and hope for the best. Schools should begin the staff recruitment process being able to name what kind of talent they are looking for.

No one goes into education to become rich and famous. Most are driven by a degree of idealism and a desire for the satisfactions of educating children and encouraging their transition into flourishing adults. For example, we strive to recruit teachers with the same degree of resilience we intend to nurture in our students.

Under any conditions, teaching is complex, demanding work. Teachers are called upon to manage through the problems kids sometimes bring to school—issues that might leave noneducators speechless. When we see up close the challenges that come with poverty—a child who comes to school hungry, a third grader who uses gang terminology—it is hard. The demands are a heavy lift. We say this out loud in the recruitment process so that candidates know what they are signing up for.

Recruiting the right talent is a job of regularly auditing the tools we use to market ourselves. If, for instance, we want to attract people who view the role of an educator as an honorable professional, yet our marketing materials contain errors or inconsistent styling, the alignment with our intention is out of whack. If our materials boast only of the joy of our school community, we are not going to attract people who will advance other elements of our vision holistically.

Go fishing where you know the fish will be attracted to your lure. Brilla's recruitment strategy includes finding graduates from colleges and universities most likely to produce people with an affinity for our vision. These include schools with a strong liberal arts or classics program. Graduates of those institutions are likely to be champions of the cardinal virtues. Similarly attractive are colleges and universities proximate to our Bronx schools. In terms of building our community from the community, it is powerful to have staff members who have shared backgrounds and experiences with the kids and families they will be serving.

All of these strategies should work in harmony to cultivate a diverse pool of staff talent who will be positioned to uplift all core elements of our vision.

Select staff for the vision.

Selection begins after recruitment. This is the moment for an organization and candidate to measure the candidate's fit—not just the person's skills and professional bona fides, but their temperamental match for the organizational culture.

Staff need to value the vision as much as any founder ever did. If they do not, if they are ambivalent toward the vision, then the match is a bad one, no matter what is on their resume. We provide ample opportunities for candidates to learn about our vision via information-rich meet-and-greet events, presence at career fairs, and other methods before they even engage in an interview process.

By design, job interviews should also be information-rich opportunities for mutual selection. By this time, the interviewer already knows what is on the resume. The interview is the opportunity to know a candidate more deeply as a prospective colleague. For the interviewee it is a chance to probe whether who they are resonates with what the school offers as a place to work. If, for example, they value silent hallways as the ideal of academic achievement, then a school like ours is not the place for them.

Ask the candidate directly, does this feel right? Do we vibe? Make the most of their outside perspective. Ask what they would change about the way the organization operates. Do not necessarily assume a new idea is fighting the vision. We need to reinforce the sincerity of our invitation to them to connect and participate by providing real-time evidence that we accept their gifts. Our talent selects us every bit as much as we select them.

As in most schools, part of our interview process is a demo lesson to see if a candidate has the skills to lead learning in the classroom. Even if a candidate excels in the demo lesson, the school might still choose not to make an offer if it gets the message that a prospect does not value a core element of our vision, such as collaboration or character formation. It is easier to coach classroom skills than it is to coach a collaborative temperament or to fight a conviction that character is merely a nice value-add for students. Without those things, the talent would be misaligned and detrimental to our vision.

Brilla also holds a culture interview conducted by peers—not by the principal but by the people with whom a candidate would be working. Broadening the group of individuals entrusted with candidate selection strengthens buy-in and reduces bias. We declare up front that this component of selection is separate from a candidate's resume or credentials. All of the questions in a culture interview are inspired by our vision for how we do school. We might ask what stood out during the school tour. What does the candidate value in a place to work? What are their goals for coaching and development? A personal favorite is, "Outside of a role in education, what is your dream job?" If our aim is to cultivate students of dynamic talents and interests, our staff members also must model that diversity of interest.

The answers to these questions will help both the candidate and us know whether what they are after is what we are offering.

The last step of selection, the reference check, can be equally intentional. Rather than checking a box, we want perspective on a candidate's greatest strengths as seen through the eyes of people who know them well. This will help us engage them immediately as participants in the school community. It will also give each of us a head start in advancing our shared goal.

The components of your selection process should attend to all the elements you consider core to your vision. Full stop. Get that wrong, and you will pay for it in attrition down the road.

Keep staff warm.

In schools, it is common for five months or more to elapse from hiring a candidate until their start date in August. If we want new hires to show up in August still eager for what we do, then we need to find ways to keep them warm, or invested.

The period between an accepted offer and the start of work in August is ripe with opportunity to start inviting staff to participate in our culture.

Soon after making an offer we send our new staff swag in a welcome box. Swag makes an immediate appeal to the heart by sending an early signal of shared identity, and it provides evidence that we use our fiscal resources to communicate value.

We invite new staff into our virtual book club.[2] Through the book club, new hires begin to bond with their new colleagues while we reinforce core elements of our vision through the books we choose. Even before they are on the payroll, new hires are contributing to our conversations.

Honoring our commitment to "extend a sincere welcome," we extend invitations to new staff members to join our end-of-year events with students and families. The intention is to create opportunities for connection. We may pair them with a staff buddy to answer questions and to provide a familiar face for when they officially report in August.

Other familiar faces will be students and staff they met during the interview process. A student from our new member's demo lesson class

[2] Amazon's senior leadership team—nicknamed the S-team—also has a book club. I like to think Brilla's is more inclusive. Taylor Soper, "Here Are the Three Amazon Execs Who Just Joined Jeff Bezos' Elite 'S-Team' Leadership Suite," *GeekWire*, August 21, 2020.

will write a handwritten note to welcome them. It is a lot more difficult for talent that has accepted an offer to ghost on a real person with whom they have established a rapport than it is when the only connection is an email address.

All this effort keeps new talent warm with micro steps aimed at increasing their commitment and driving their excitement before they arrive for their first day.

Onboard for staff commitment.

Just prior to the start of the school year new staff and returning staff alike participate in at least two weeks of onboarding. Any school's onboarding should be bigger than just training and orientation. In our case the primary goal of onboarding is to deepen staff's under-standing of and appreciation for both the school model and for the school community—essentially, for our vision. Onboarding is a critical and immersive experience into the way we do things.

In a way, this two-week period is structured much like this book. We start by immersing staff in the rich details of our vision, as viscerally as we can. Students and their families participate as guest speakers. We want staff—especially new staff—to see and hear how families feel about a Brilla education and how it comes to life for them. Their stories tug at our heartstrings. We complement this by sharing data from the previous school year as further—empirical—evidence of our program's impact. It provides rational appeal.

Our launch sessions are a critical tool for communications. We explicitly emphasize the benefits and expectations of membership in our school community. We have sessions on professionalism, family engagement, how to facilitate virtue formation, and excellent academic instruction for kids. Once a new teacher is assigned to a class, they will start to form bonds with students, and families will be counting on them. If we are not feeling like the right place for them, this is the time to say so before our train leaves the station.

The invitation to embrace our shared identity is extended during this period by explicit introduction to our rituals and traditions. A symbolic song starts playing, or our mascot emerges, and we present more swag.

We practice our concern for engagement via frequent and purposeful opportunities for staff to connect, participate, and share their gifts. Time and treasure are spent on strengthening the understanding of all the parts of our school model, in large groups and small groups, within and across campuses. Staff members present their life maps and launch virtual gatherings we call Brilla Bunches.

Then we prime for execution. Our approach models what it looks like to build anticipation. We plan in detail to maximize the impact of every session, of every coffee break, of every email. We serve as active hosts for our newest team members. They learn and practice how to launch their Brilla career by participating experientially in an immersion in our daily schedule, collaborating around how they will affirm and develop the talents of our students. We tie it all in a bow with an inspiring video to reflect on and relive all that we have accomplished together in just two short weeks, even before the purpose for our work, the children, have set foot in the building.

If the commitment isn't there by the end of our staff onboarding experience, it probably isn't ever going to be. Assuming it is, we turn our attention to how to keep the magic alive as the ebbs and flows of a school year get underway.

Coach staff constantly.

If we believe in dignified engagement, then we cannot treat talent like cogs in a machine. Saying this out loud should begin even before people climb aboard the train.

Even great talent needs a clear frame for what excellence looks like. Then there is an opportunity for school leadership to partner them with a coach who will help guide the path to excellence. We set a high bar and celebrate when staff rise to it, making course adjustments along the way.

Any job demands role and behavior competencies for success. Naturally, operations team members and teachers have different role competencies, or skills required to be successful in their job. For a teacher these might include abilities in lesson execution, classroom management, love and logic, or rigor. For an operations team member they might include facilities maintenance, safety, or record keeping.

Behavior competencies, by contrast, are common to everyone—or should be. They are the performance aspects that support the culture we are building, the social and professional behaviors we want staff to model for the rest of the community. We expect everyone to be competent in communication, family relationships, constant learning, and participation in school events. To keep courting our talent, an effective coach will keep all of these elements top of mind when shaping coaching conversations and development plans on an ongoing basis.

Regardless of role, we strive for a biweekly cycle of observing staff performance. We provide written feedback aligned to established objectives. We discuss this feedback one on one in large part to practice the next right move.

Then we go and apply the feedback. And the cycle repeats.

Coaching should be continual. We would not ask staff to wait for an annual review any more than we would give students their first piece of formal feedback at report card conferences. We discuss progress continually so that staff members always know whether they are approaching, meeting, or exceeding standards. It sends a signal to staff that the organization is routinely invested in their success, not just when the calendar calls for it.

Finally, the most transformative coaching is strength-based. The message should be explicit: "Here is what you are doing well, and here is how you can leverage that strength to grow in your role." When done well, that will make the next step, evaluation, simply a formal stamp on an ongoing coaching conversation.

Evaluate staff against the vision.

Formal evaluations represent a moment in time when we can zoom out and assess performance holistically, anchored in evidence obtained through the ongoing coaching cycle. However, if our goal is for all stakeholders to be integral and mutually accountable to fulfilling the vision, then it stands to reason that they should have a say on whether others are meeting the expectations we all signed up for. One tool for this can be a 360-degree performance review.[3] In a 360-degree review, performance feedback is solicited from around the organization—supervisors, peers, and subordinates alike. At our school we also include families. And at the middle school level, student feedback is invited as well. The idea of a 360-degree review is to give the person receiving it a perspective on how their contributions are viewed by the total organization. It also provides a unique value-add to evaluations to distinguish them from routine coaching conversations.

In conducting staff evaluations, we pay attention to progress in professional development, rookies and veterans alike, across all the elements of our vision that we claim to care about. No one in an organization can be allowed to plateau. If we believe this about our kids, then we must believe it about ourselves and our teams.

Recruit families for the vision.

Here is something that may surprise you: all the talent development practices we employ with staff are transferable to the other talent in a school community—students and their families.

Again, families in our community have choices for educating their children. If families do not choose us, we have no school. So, we recruit as many families as we can; we want to fill every seat and offer a Brilla education to as many children as possible. We want families in our community to know that a Brilla education is available to them, so

---

[3] Jack Zenger and Joseph Folkman, "What Makes a 360-Degree Review Successful?" *Harvard Business Review*, December 23, 2020.

they can discern whether a Brilla education is what they desire for their child.

Our vision is to be a community school, so we begin by prioritizing marketing in our local neighborhood. And as we do in recruiting staff, we audit our marketing materials that target families against the core tenets of our vision.

If the whole person is central to our vision, do our materials tell that story? If all our materials portray pictures of children sitting with their hands folded, then what story are we telling about ourselves? Because we cherish intellectual growth, we incorporate photos of our scholars on computers engaged in blended learning with a teacher at a U-shaped table, or reading independently. Our marketing materials also show students laughing with their friends, practicing fine arts, demonstrating one of our virtues by performing on stage (courage), and campaigning for student council (justice). That sends the message that our vision is a balanced one. It targets the families for which our vision is resonant.

We partner with local businesses and ask them to post our materials. This is not a passive pursuit. This is a partnership. In exchange for telling customers about us, small businesses get the word out about themselves. The partnership has now evolved into a full-fledged campaign called Bronx Educated, led by a pioneering Brilla leader, Reyes Claudio.

Several years ago, a start-up in our Mott Haven neighborhood, Empanology, agreed to put up our flyers. We repaid the favor by sometimes ordering their (fantastic) empanadas for our gatherings. Now that Empanology has found its feet and is drawing attention from New York foodies,[4] it still puts up our flyers. In its window sits our plush red bird.

---

[4] Ben Miller, "Empanology to Provide Food at the Bronx Brewery," *New York Business Journal*, September 18, 2020.

We also cultivate a presence at community centers, local churches, and pre-kindergartens. We invite the pre-Ks, for example, to bring their kids on field trips to our schools. Then—we hope—the kids will go home and talk about how they met our nice teachers and our big red bird. As a result, our demand for seats exceeds seats available by more than three times.

Empower families to select for the vision.

We do not select families in the same sense that we select staff. While we intend to emphasize mutual choice in both cases, Brilla ultimately has final say in staff selection, whereas families have ultimate say in school selection. What is the same is that even before families enter the spring lottery, we provide an information-rich preview of what our school is all about. We do this to emphasize choice. Our method is via an open house.

The open house is usually the first time families have encountered our vision for our school beyond our modest marketing efforts and word-of-mouth in the neighborhood.

To put a human face on that vision, the panel we assemble for the open house includes current family members and staff. They are not there for decoration. Staff are there to say what it is like to work at the school. Families are there to share their experiences. Stakeholders outside of formal leadership speak with a different kind of credibility about the vision and what the experience of joining the community will be like. We want prospective families to hear what they are signing up for from the people with whom they will become friends and partners for the next ten years.

Soon after acceptances go out, we hold a celebration to which we invite new students and their parents. We signal with great pride that they have selected our school community. Their names are read aloud, and they have their picture taken with the mascot. We offer uniform fittings to engineer anticipation for the moment when they can proudly display their membership as a Brilla student.

And once again we seize the opportunity to tell everyone what they are signing up for.

Keep families warm.

If we want new students and families to show up in August still eager for what we do, then we need to find ways to keep them warm, the same as we do with new staff.

Not long after the admissions celebration we start home visits. Nothing we do sends a more serious signal about our idea of community than these visits. We offer home visits for new families and for families sending another sibling to school the next year.

Usually, the kids are almost overcome with excitement (though some may be a little shy) at the appearance of someone from their new school. They are presented with a Brilla T-shirt—the first visible sign that they have stepped aboard our train. They are on their way.

During home visits we get insight into what an individual child is bringing to school from their first five years of life. Who do they live with? What do they enjoy? We are beginning the work of partnering with families on how to give our best to their child.

In the home visit we outline the community's expectations, as we will do again and again in the coming years. We explain that we expect children to come to school every day. We expect students in uniform because they are part of a community that is instilling an identity of self-care and professionalism. If children are sick, we expect parents to call us. During the year we expect parents to volunteer for at least one of our events. We understand that parents may not be able to help a student with their homework, though we expect them to provide a dedicated space where their child can study.

We name all the things we bring to the partnership: frequent, transparent, personalized communication; justice and empathy when responding to challenging situations; professionalism and personal care; a high-quality curriculum coupled with excellent individualized instruction; teachers who will love their child as their own.

After home visits it is a long way to our August start, especially for five-year-olds. During that intervening period we want to keep up our new students' excitement as well.

We pump up shared identity as much as we can. We blitz the kids with Brilla-branded items. In early summer we send students a package that includes a coloring book featuring the main events that happen throughout the school year, such as the Mott Haven Celebration, Costume Carnival, talent show, our mock Winter Olympics, and so on. Each page of the coloring book includes a little explanation. All of it is a way of saying, "We are still thinking about you and we are still excited that you are coming." It reinforces what they have signed up for while building anticipation.

All the while we are crystal clear with families about what engagement with the school community will require. They can still say no.

Onboard for family commitment.

Back-to-school nights are commonplace. The good ones should be analogous to onboarding for staff.

The tone of our back-to-school night in mid-August is meant to convey our passion about the specifics of our vision. For new families, this will be their deepest dive yet into our vision for the program.

Just as staff onboarding is a new hire's last chance to say, "This is not my train," the same is true for families at back-to-school night. We make it plain that if they are having second thoughts about Brilla, it is OK to choose a different school. We tell parents to not send their kids to our school if it does not seem like the best fit for their child or their family, but to please make that decision before their child arrives and starts making friends and connecting with their teacher.

You might think this strange. What other organization would allow prospective customers to walk away? By stressing that joining our school is a process of mutual discernment, we deepen the buy-in to our vision.

We want families to be as intentional about the choice they are making as staff are when they decide to come aboard.

Evaluate students against the vision.

The concepts of coaching and evaluation may be a stretch in their application to families, but the process is integral to students.

Our vision for students is one of constant growth and learning, of holistic development. Therefore it is our duty to coach for all of these elements in harmony and balance, whether through written feedback on an assignment, rigorous questioning during instruction, or empowering conversations during life's teachable moments. All of these coaching methods occur on a regular basis, for all students.

Our formal evaluation structure for students—report cards—must similarly have alignment to convey that all of the core elements of our vision matter. Our report cards include academic indicators, of course, but also evaluations for fine and applied arts, character, and social-emotional learning. A supporting narrative speaks to the rich gifts students bring, the contributions they make to their classroom community, and the just-right next steps to further their achievement. They are informed by the classroom teacher as well as by other educators with whom the student frequently engages to promote a complete and balanced snapshot of student performance.

If it seems I am starting to repeat myself, it's because I am, not only in this particular chapter, but in the book as a whole. The through line is intentionality, alignment from vision to engagement to execution, for every practice, for every stakeholder. A virtuous circle of clarity and consistency, anchored in a powerfully appealing purpose, is what compels people to go all in for outcomes.

And the people are indispensable. After all, the outcomes for students are facilitated through people, the adults who teach them and the parents with whom they partner. Even an incredibly well-designed school model will flop, never achieving enduring high performance, if the leaders who shepherd it do not win the hearts and minds of those who facilitate the vision—staff—and those for whom it is intended—the students and families.

Ask anyone, young or old, to tell you about their education, and before long they will be talking about the people met in school, teachers and peers alike—the ones who brought them joy and those who brought them misery. Ask anyone about the jobs they have had later in life, or the institutions and communities they have been part of, and their reflections will be a version of the same.

People work for people. (And I don't mean that strictly in the hierarchical sense.) Every step described in this book returns to that truth.

The people we learn with and work with teach us lessons that stick with us all our lives. When the experience reaches our hearts and minds, we are *all in*.

. . . .

REFLECT ON YOUR PRACTICE

Recruit for the vision.

- How does your vision inform your understanding of what constitutes a great fit in your talent landscape?

- How does your vision inform your recruitment materials?

- How does your vision inform the target market for your recruitment efforts and guide you on where to source talent?

Select for the vision.

- How do your selection processes provide information-rich exposure to the vision?

- How do the interview components you employ during staff selection attend to all elements that are core to the vision?

Keep them warm.

- How do you engage with stakeholders during the interval of time between making a commitment to join the school community and their actual start date?

- How do your practices engage stakeholders and expose them to core elements of your vision?

Onboard for commitment.

- How does your vision inform each aspect of your onboarding program?

- How does your onboarding experience apply each step described in this book to maximize the potential for full buy-in to your vision?

- Where are there synergies between the onboarding experience you craft for staff and the one you craft for students and families?

Coach constantly.

- How does the frequency of your coaching structures ensure ongoing growth and development for stakeholders?

- How does your coaching method reinforce all aspects that are core to your vision, including both skills and behaviors?

Evaluate against the vision.

- How does your formal evaluation process align with the ongoing coaching that talent receives?

- How are you leveraging the perspectives of other stakeholders to ensure a more complete and balanced performance assessment?

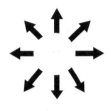

Growth and Other Good Problems to Have

Neville Teagarden, an investor in advanced technologies like artificial intelligence, has a rule about getting involved in young companies: no heroes.

Hero culture is what you get when an organization comes to believe that its charismatic founder is indispensable. "But hero culture doesn't scale," says Teagarden. "If something happens to the hero the whole thing fails."[1] The mark of a leader is of someone who can build an organization that will thrive and grow when the founders are gone.

In 2015, founding principal Aaron Gillaspie left Brilla to raise his family in another city. I was asked to become principal. Saying I had mixed emotions at the departure of my friend and co-founder is putting

---

[1] L. Kevin Kelly, John F. Mulholland, and Kevin McDermott, *Paragraph 3: Conversations about Prepared Leadership in the Age of Perpetual Uncertainty—from the C-Suite to the Battlefield.* (Page Publishing, 2022).

it mildly. Being director of community and culture for the flagship Brilla school had been my favorite job ever. Now I was going to oversee the whole program—academics, character, operations, you name it. I was being asked to oversee and uplift the entirety of the vision. I took the job because I was eager to grow our network of schools and, along with them, the influence of the Brilla vision in the wider community.

And Brilla grew. It was proof that if vision, engagement, and execution are methodically applied across the organization, success will never be dependent on one person.

Growth complexifies the execution of a vision. But not the "why" of that vision. If it is to have continued success, a school needs to acknowledge this difference out loud. When I left Brilla, I was never more convinced of anything than I was of the rightness of that conviction.

I left Brilla even as I was still learning how to be good at my job, but with confidence that the vision, and the culture that was born from it, will endure. I could not leave without telling the story of its creation and the formation of that culture. That story deserves to be told, and I want to help others learn from it.

In many ways it will be harder for my successors than it was for me and for other members of the founding team. They will have the challenge of sustaining the intense commitment felt by the early investors in the Brilla vision. An expanding community of students, families, and staff—individually terrific in brand-new ways—will soon have little personal memory of our formational experience. They will have to rely more on the collected memory handed down through stories, traditions, and artifacts like this book. Yet recollection alone will be insufficient to win their hearts and minds. It will take persistent attention to the steps I have laid out, as well as specific attention to the challenges of growth.

Tend to hierarchical and physical distance.

As an organization begins to grow, two things that buoy its success in the beginning will not be sustainable. The first, of course, is the inspirational founding leader, standing on the sidewalk handing leaflets to passersby.

The second is that when an organization is young and small, the people working in it are most likely the same people shaping its vision and taking an active role in execution. The organization can almost—*almost*—get away without having to work on buy-in. Buy-in can be assumed. Everyone in the building shows up for work already bought in.

In Brilla's first two years the gap between vision and execution was almost nothing. With growth came interesting kinds of problems to have, such as the risk of a gap between vision and execution, between the school and the community it intends to serve, between centralized leaders and on-the-ground practitioners. Those gaps can threaten the success that brought growth in the first place.

When I consider the principal problems of growth, it seems they divide into the challenges of space: literal physical space and the metaphorical space between people and the vision.

All of us at Brilla are proud of our growth from two grades in an old building in 2013 to five schools across the Bronx in 2022. That growth was a ratification of the vision we had in 2013, back when we were standing on street corners and hoping to entice families to a school that was not yet open. But I admit that following the through line from vision to engagement to execution was easier when we were small.

In our first year of operation, Brilla had two grades and twelve teachers. When we needed to come together and brainstorm, our whole staff of twenty or so could sit in one classroom. It was easy for us all to be on the same page, and easy to know it when we were not. By the time we grew to four grades, the risk of gears slipping was becoming apparent.

For example, as we grew we had to address the very human feelings among the founding team who realized they were no longer in every meeting. They could not help wondering whether they continued to be as central to shaping the school's vision as they had been. It would have been easy for these folks to disengage, to feel a little angry at what might appear to be a diminished place in the culture.

For people new to the organization, the risk was that they felt no buy-in at all. They had no idea of the "why" of our vision because we had not yet learned how to tell them, again and again, what they had signed up for and the integral role they had to play in building the organization. In pursuit of execution, we were not as smart as we would later become about engagement.

Additionally, communication among the nodes in the network began to resemble a big game of telephone. Everyone spun even good ideas according to their own perspective. Key details got lost. This is one more reason to be supremely clear about what all the members of the community are signing up for—the "why" of the vision, in other words, and how it is supported by operational practice across the whole organization and not just in its parts.

In 2017, the year Brilla grew from one school to three, we had an advantage in that all three principals of our schools had been members of the founding team. We took for granted that of course they understood the "why" of our vision. And yet that first physical separation of our schools already gave small early warnings that cracks might appear in our shared identity. For a simple example, the way our elementary and middle schools were each interpreting our "all black shoes" policy for student dress code turned into an unexpectedly big ordeal. A parent who had siblings enrolled in each was told by one school that her child's shoes were out of compliance, and by the other that they were fine. It was a bad look for us and a source of immense frustration for the parent.

The more any organization grows, the greater the risk of distance between the people making final decisions and the people implementing them. Speaking for myself, there were times in my last several years at Brilla when I worried that I was not appropriately in touch with what principals were experiencing.

When we were a small organization, tension points were necessarily limited in number. Fewer people and less complexity elicited fewer organizational challenges. Now Brilla has grown to five schools, with an intention of building three more. The school network is so much larger. Now, instead of one person in each domain, there is a team. And every member of the team expects to have input when resolving problems.

Such are the problems of success.

Fight the temptation to silo.

In the spring of 2020, we faced a challenge none of us had ever contemplated: school that was not happening in the building. Overnight, unfamiliar complexity touched every single member of the organization. It was a kind of founding experience all over again, in miniature.

In the early days of our organization, we responded to unfamiliar complexity by committing to distributed leadership. We knew from our beginnings how individual commitment to the vision produced the success of all of us together. That supplied the logic of cascading influence at each level of leadership, straight through to the teacher in the classroom.

Following that logic, it was inevitable that eight years later we would be evaluating school principals not merely on how well their school performed, but on how their leadership supported the healthy growth of the entire network. That evaluation metric was an intentional vision-aligned structure meant to encourage cross-campus collaboration to solve common problems, such as re-envisioning our school model during COVID-19, rather than retreating in isolation to problem-solve.

There seems to be a perverse desire in growing organizations to split into silos based on job description or simply on location. Functionally, it feels logical. But the tendency fights cross-group intimacy and undermines engagement.

A simple example of this tendency toward siloing is Brilla's annual holiday party for staff. It is a large event at which we get to meet and form friendships with members of the organization with whom we might otherwise never connect. As Brilla grew, I sometimes heard pushback from people who support the value of connection but feel the holiday event should be organized according to campus. Bearing in mind our vision of cross-campus partnership and genuine connection, I put my foot down. That event is one of our few remaining opportunities to remind everyone that we are engaged in shared work and that our impact is stronger together, and we need to celebrate it.

Or consider the issue of test preparation for state achievement exams. Differing perspectives on the right way to do test prep have at times arisen between our centralized academic leaders and our network of principals. Both parties have deep expertise. Both have smart teams backing them up. Such tensions are confirmation of the power in ensuring that everyone feels responsibility for high performance.

The dialogue is good. The job of leadership is to assure that the dialogue is aligned with the non-negotiables in our vision.

Nourishing the conditions of connection and participation takes more time than conventional command-and-control models of leadership. It would be so much easier to just tell people what to do. But in our case, the outcome would not be human flourishing, nor would it be organizational growth.

Do not throttle innovation.

The risk hidden in rigorously codifying organizational practice is that an organization might end up throttling innovation precisely because its practices have brought success in the past. In pursuit of engagement, it might end up sending a message that says, "This is how you must do things. You must never vary from these rules."

Candor about the continued suitability of our practice to our vision is essential. As someone once remarked, "The greatest danger in times of turbulence is not the turbulence, it's acting with yesterday's logic."[2]

---

[2] This statement has been widely attributed to management guru and author Peter Drucker, though he wasn't the first to use it. The original quote's source is unknown.

In education, the name of the game is adaptation. I cannot think of an enterprise in the twenty-first century for which adaptation is not the name of the game. The challenge of adaptation will be to keep growing in our practice without missing signals from the community telling us when it is time to evolve.

No enterprise should ever believe it has created the perfect formula and that all it needs to do is keep executing against that. I hope no one I work with ever believes that. Too many organizations cling to operational structures that have brought them success in the past beyond the point where those structures no longer deliver on the vision.

Let me be the first to say that it is a special risk for successful founders to want to control an organization from the afterlife by leaving behind a list of commandments. (And though I see how you could perceive this book to be just that, my hope is to provide context for the "what" and "why" rather than compelling the "how.")

Our annual Costume Carnival, hosted by the flagship Brilla school, has the intention of providing not only an enjoyable time, but also fostering the full engagement of all the members of our community—students, families, staff. In our first year of growth beyond a single school building, one of our culture leads proposed eliminating costumes from the fall celebration at their school and rebranding the event as a fall festival. It surprised me how resistant I was to these changes. Was I being a control-freak founder?

Yes, partially.

Had I been insistent on my way of doing things, I stood a good chance of sending a message that innovation was not wanted. I might have thwarted the sense of investment in our practice among new staff. Then I remembered that what matters most about our fall event is that it supports the vision of community building, that it be open to siblings, and that it be held at a time convenient for working families. Those are nonnegotiable. Nowhere in there does it say anything about wearing costumes.

It was a good example of striking a balance between vision in the network and an individual school's autonomy. That realization was an important moment in the evolution of our practice. In retrospect it advanced the organization's thinking about distributed leadership and how to ensure clear boundaries around autonomy.

To feel fully engaged in organizational growth, talent needs to be empowered with a sense of personal agency guided by the elements of the vision. Without that full engagement the best talents will disengage and grab the first good opportunity to depart. When we need them, they will not be around.

There will be tensions that come with growth, certainly, but they are good tensions to have. Getting the management of the tensions right is an ongoing conversation. It was not so hard when we were smaller. As more smart people climb aboard our train, the greater the challenge of creative tensions will be.

And that is all right. Without creative tension, neither the vision nor the innovations that advance the vision could thrive.

Never lose sight of the vision.

When Brilla opened, every one of us had skin in the game. We had staff who had left other jobs to join us. We had families who were betting on the education of the children they brought to school that first day. We had to succeed. There was no backup plan. However much we grow, none of that should ever change.

If my successors were to ask my advice, I would remind them that the vision transcends all of us. They should accept with gratitude all the gifts of all the people on the train. To do anything else would be contrary to our beliefs about the essential role of people.

My successors and their successors are likely to have to-do lists that I cannot imagine. It is quite likely that when I come back to Brilla in fifteen years I will recognize that the vision we had in 2013 was right for the time, but the time has changed, and the vision and its supports in the form of engagement and execution need to reflect that.

In pursuit of a vision, what matters most is not the successes of the past. It is the sustained intention behind what the organization does next.

An organizational culture should never be finished. It should evolve as the community it serves evolves and as the greater context in which it operates evolves. It should reflect, learn about itself, and adapt. The members of the organization should always be working to make it a little more right.

It is easy to lose track of the intentions at the heart of any organization when you are caught up in the day-to-day of getting tasks completed. Our organization, for example, is learning to track the impact of our vision on students and their families. Our schools are not yet ten years old, and already we are thinking about creating structures to support an alumni network for our students who have graduated on to high school. This would be a logical buildout of our existing structures of connection.

In the meantime, for homecoming week we have our fifth graders come back to their elementary school as returning alumni. They sing the old songs and chants with the younger kids to prove they still know them. It is an affirmation of a shared connection across grades and across years. By going back, the middle schoolers are modeling the success of the vision to the younger kids (chiefly by relating how cool middle school is). We want to stay in active touch with our students, and they with us.

Live the engaged life.

The ancient Greeks believed that the path to happiness was a meaningful life, which for them was the feeling we derive from being part of something bigger than ourselves.[3] Susan David, a founder of the Harvard/McLean Institute of Coaching and a member of the Harvard

---

[3] Susan David, "How Happy Is Your Organization?" *Harvard Business Review*, March 20, 2013.

Medical School faculty, points out that one of the ancient Greek words for happiness is "eudaimonia," which roughly translates as "the engaged life."[4]

For the Greeks, the engaged life referred to a person's ability to deploy their personal genius. It is from the accumulation of our efforts to achieve eudaimonia in initiatives large and small that we make our lives thrive and cause our cultures to adapt. The closer we come to realizing the goal of an engaged life, the more our initiatives will make an impact that sticks.

A thriving school does not just happen because well-intentioned people wish for it. Nor is a great school made during onboarding or in a single all-hands event. A thriving culture is built every day and reinforced when we seize even small opportunities to be intentional and to win the full engagement of the people.

---

[4] Susan David, Emotional Agility: Get Unstuck, Embrace Change, and Thrive in Work and Life (Avery, 2016).

Gratitude

Consider this book a 200-page love letter to all the students, families and staff at Brilla Public Charter Schools. They made the Brilla success story. They epitomize *all in.*

There is no one to whom I owe more than the children entrusted to Brilla's care. Every morning when I came into work their faces, the twinkle in their eyes, gave me a jolt of adrenaline that carried me through even the hardest day. I am forever grateful to them for showing me what a gift an all-consuming purpose in life can be. It is an honor to serve as a mentor.

Here is a thing to know about mentors: They make a choice to believe in you. They are not required to. They do not have to see your potential just because they spend time with you. And yet they do. On days when I was full of doubt my mentors kept my belief in myself alive. They helped me see things I did not realize were there.

Easily dozens of individuals have served as mentors and shaped my thinking about what makes a great school organization. Some are called out by name in the chapters of *All In*. Many are not. Though it is impractical to list all of them, it does not make their impact any less.

Stephanie Saroki de Garcia, managing director of Seton Education Partners, was a Brilla co-founder. It was her vision to create a classically-inspired charter-school model to serve families impacted by the shuttering of Catholic schools. Stephanie and I have often joked that Brilla was her baby but she entrusted it to me to raise. Her trust gave me the platform to put my gifts to work.

Luanne Zurlo is the executive director of the Brilla Schools Network. When I told Luanne that I wanted to write a book about all we learned in the near-decade since Brilla opened she not only encouraged me but provided the resources to make it happen. Luanne is a person of generous spirit, and without her tangible support I am not sure *All In* would have materialized.

Deborah Redmond has followed my leadership journey since my first days as a school principal. As a mentor and leadership coach, she knows perhaps better than anyone what it took for me to overcome self-doubt, learn from my mistakes, and aspire to level five leadership. And she helped me to do so. Kevin McDermott allowed me to speak freely about every transformative experience, to harness the lessons learned so they could be shared with clarity on these pages. On my darkest days working on this book a call with them reinvigorated and reaffirmed my confidence that I had something to offer. Without them there were times when I might have stopped writing.

Writing, after all, is a way of exposing yourself, at least if you are writing honestly. The people I asked to review *All In* when it was still in manuscript were trusted confidantes, the ones I counted on to tell me the good, the bad, the ugly even when it made me squirm. One of them was Matt Larsen, a founding staff member at Brilla who knows our story from its beginning. Matt was right in the middle of every transition I made at Brilla. Matt is a friend and a colleague, and he stood by me when I wondered if I had the chops to be in a leadership role.

Michael Carbone was Brilla's chief academic officer. Mike joined the team at a time when growth was making it obvious that my role was too much for one person to handle. Sharing authority that had previously been mine alone could have been a scary thing. Instead, Mike became my work husband: we argued sometimes but ultimately we care about each other and wanted to do our best for the schools.

Ali Apfel was Brilla's assistant principal when I was principal and subsequently succeeded me in that role. Along the way she became my great friend. She seems to know what I am thinking before I say it out loud and pushes me to make my thinking stronger. I trust her to be a foil for even my most far-out ideas. She has never ceased to be my partner.

I was privileged to be raised by parents who cultivated an environment where it never occurred to me that I could not do something. Their fingerprints are all over my educational philosophy. They told me out loud and on purpose that if I wanted to do a thing I would find a way. They instilled in me a no-nonsense confidence. Every day that I have worked in schools I've wanted that kind of unadulterated confidence to take root in our kids.

My mother, and my grandmother Gam, are the kind of women who seem to be everything to anybody who needs them. When I assumed my first leadership role, theirs was the example I pulled from. There were so many things that threatened my sense of competence, so much to hold together. My mother and Gam gave me the model I needed, not least their insistence on paying attention to all the details.

More than once people have said to me, "Kelsey, you look like your mom but you act exactly like your dad." My dad taught me about being all in. On the day I was married my father did not simply toast to my happiness. Instead, he rapped a father-of-the-bride song, encouraging the guests to sing along. Right there you have at least three different elements of this book: facilitate connection, invite participation, and ensure impact. My dad is a constant model of how to make the most of any situation and maximize the engagement you get out of it.

At the top of my personal mountain of gratitude is my husband, Chris. Apart from me Chris has the most sweat equity in the book you are reading. His comments on the draft were 99 percent on the money, even when at times I did not want to hear them. If I had any chance of taking this book from good to great I needed Chris. He is all in for ensuring my success, all the while managing to be all in for his own career and pursuits, all in as a husband, and all in as a loving father to our silver lab and two spirited girls. I knew what I was signing up for when I chose him as my life partner, and it's even better than the vision he sold me on.

All these people brought me gifts, and I accepted them. To anyone who has ever been all in for me or all in for Brilla, I credit you for this work. You have my deepest, heartfelt gratitude.

Index

CPSIA information can be obtained
at www.ICGtesting.com
Printed in the USA
BVHW030128060722
641400BV00003B/8/J

9 781737 288688